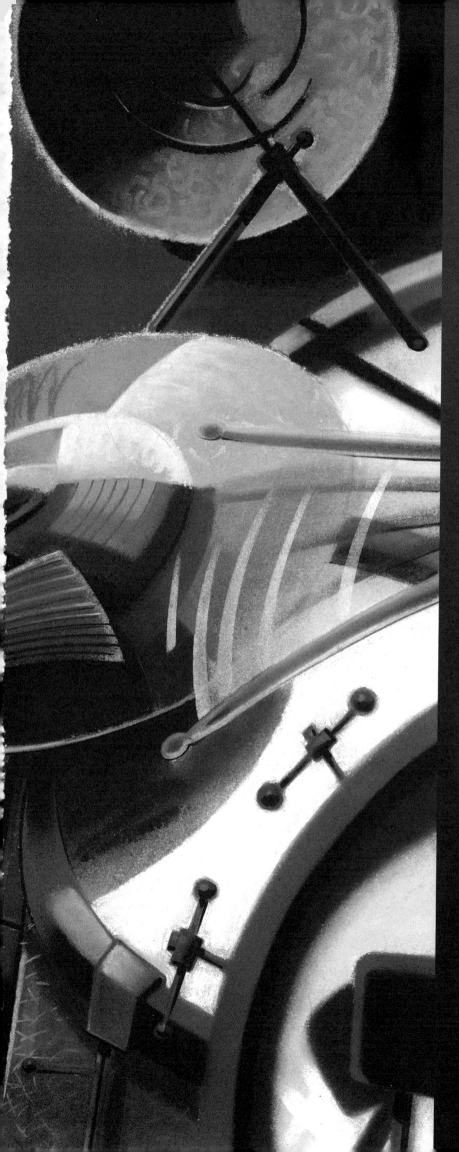

Incl...

LEA...
DRUMSET

ALL-IN-ONE COMBO PACK

Complete Instruction from Beginner to Advanced

by Peter Magadini

About the Audio and Video

To access all of the audio tracks and videos that accompany this book, simply go to **www.halleonard.com/mylibrary** and enter the code found here. The music examples and sections that include audio and video are marked with icons throughout the book.

To access online content visit:
www.halleonard.com/mylibrary

Enter Code
1815-8405-4076-8159

PLAYBACK+
Speed • Pitch • Balance • Loop

ISBN 978-1-4950-8876-6

7777 W. BLUEMOUND RD. P.O. BOX 13819 MILWAUKEE, WI 53213

Copyright © 1980, 1999, 2017 by HAL LEONARD LLC
International Copyright Secured All Rights Reserved

No part of this publication may be reproduced in any form or
by any means without the prior written permission of the Publisher.

In Australia Contact:
Hal Leonard Australia Pty. Ltd.
4 Lentara Court
Cheltenham, Victoria, 3192 Australia
Email: ausadmin@halleonard.com.au

Visit Hal Leonard Online at
www.halleonard.com

DEDICATION

This book is dedicated to the memory of Niko Magadini.

Peter would like to thank everyone at Hal Leonard who helped make this book possible: Keith Mardak, Jeff Schroedl, Richard Slater, Kurt Plahna, Steve Jaeger, and Kristen Anhalt.

INTRODUCTION

Perhaps you're a young aspiring newcomer to music, or maybe an experienced musician whose passion for the drums has finally pushed you into purchasing a complete drumset. Whatever the reason for your decision to study the drums, you've chosen an instrument that is extremely versatile and one that is heard almost daily by anyone exposed to music. Drums and drummers have been around since man first hit a log with a stick and the art of playing the instrument has expanded and matured to a level that makes drums one of the most popular instruments in the world.

This book was written to teach you the basics of the drumset in the shortest amount of time and will explain how the drumset functions in many styles of contemporary music. In addition to learning the basics of reading and improvisation, you'll also learn the coordination of hands and feet... all in a practical but fun-filled manner. So, if you're learning on your own or with the help of a teacher, the results will be an exciting and rewarding musical experience.

CONTENTS

DRUMSET BASICS ▶

For many years, the basic drumset consisted of four drums: the bass drum, the rack or mounted tom-tom (or high tom-tom), the floor tom-tom (or low tom-tom), and the snare drum.

Basic Four Piece Setup

Rack Tom-Tom

Snare Drum

Bass Drum

Floor Tom-Tom

Hi-Hat Pedal

Bass Drum Pedal

Many drums (including an additional bass drum) can be added to a basic setup. However, it's my opinion that adding drums at a later stage of development is much less of a problem once you learn to master various techniques on a basic setup. Therefore, I've designed the contents of this book to generally apply to either the basic four piece or basic five piece drumset.

Basic Five Piece Setup

Tuning (Tensioning) the Drumset

Most drums are not actually tuned to a specific pitch. If they were, they'd have to be retuned with each different piece or even every change of chord. They are tuned (some drummers prefer the term "tensioned") so that the drums being played range from higher to lower without emphasis being placed on actual pitches.

The following **instructions** explain how to tune the bass drum. The same procedure should be followed for all the other drums. Keep in mind that the tom-toms are tensioned so they sound from high to low as you move from left to right while playing. The snare drum, as a rule, is tensioned tighter than the bass drum and the tom-toms.

Clockwise, work your way around the drum turning each tuning rod a few times. Do this until the head becomes evenly tensioned all the way around (there should be no ripples anywhere on the surface).

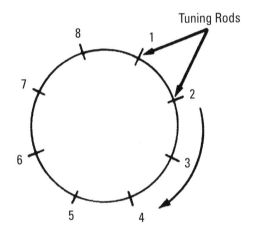

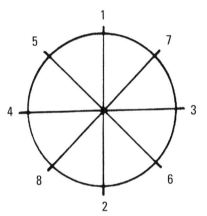

You may also gain the same results by criss-cross tuning.

When the head is sufficiently tight, take one hand and put it palm down in the middle of the drum head. Place the other hand on top and press firmly on the head with both hands. Do not be disturbed if you hear a cracking or popping sound. This is merely the new head adjusting itself to the added tension. Once this is done, the head will hold the tension consistently wherever you set it. This is called **seating the head**. As stated previously, **the same procedure should be followed on all drum heads**.

Arranging Your Set

Now that you've tuned your drums, it will be necessary to set them up so that you can achieve the maximum results with the minimum amount of motion. Since no two drummers are the same shape or size, here are some simple suggestions to follow:

- Adjust your seat so that your legs are straight out from your hips and are parallel to the floor. Your knees should be bent at approximately a 90° angle and your feet should feel comfortable on the pedals. (Your left foot should be on the hi-hat pedal and your right foot on the bass drum foot pedal.)*

- The snare drum should be directly in front of you and approximately belt buckle high.

- The rack tom-tom should be above and to the left of the snare drum. It should be tilted downward toward the snare drum at a 40° angle.

NOTE: If two rack tom-toms are used, the second one should also tilt toward the snare drum.

- The floor tom should be placed as close as possible to your bass drum leg and just a bit lower than the height of the snare drum.

- The hi-hat cymbals should be set 6 to 10 inches higher than the snare drum. The space between the hi-hat cymbals should be approximately 1/2 to 1 inch.

- The stands which hold the ride cymbal and crash cymbal should be placed as closely to the set as possible and approximately 6 to 12 inches above the rack tom-toms. The cymbals should tilt a bit toward the snare drum head. They must be close enough to reach with ease but not so close that they interfere with the sticks as you maneuver around the set.

*Opposite for left-handed drummer

The Electronic Drumset

In the beginning, some drummers might consider substituting an electronic drumset over the acoustic drumset. You certainly can go a long way when learning how to play the drums with just this instrument. Also, if sound in your living space is an issue, this works as an acceptable alternative. Drummers who might be playing in bands or with other acoustic instrumentalists naturally prefer the acoustic drumset, while perhaps employing the electronic set mainly for practice at home or studio. If you have your choice of only one or the other, it is strongly suggested to start on the acoustic drumset.

The Practice Pad

The practice pad and the electronic drumset are logical substitutes for the real thing. In many cases, practice on the live set is impractical or impossible due to the close proximity of neighbors and family. Therefore, a practice pad set may be a necessary practicing tool depending upon your own personal situation.

The Drumstick

Nylon Tip   Wood Tip

The drumstick is your tool. Without it, drumset playing as we know it would be impossible. If possible, I suggest you get some professional help in picking out the proper drumsticks for your hand. If no professional help is available, try to find drumsticks of a medium weight. Roll the sticks on the countertop to make sure they are not warped. A straight stick is an absolute requirement for maximum playing results. You may also want to tap the sticks on a hard surface to check for consistency in sound.

Holding the Sticks

The first decision you have to make as a new drummer is which grip to use to hold the sticks. There are two: the traditional grip (also called the "over and under grip") and the matched grip. Following is an explanation of both.

The Traditional Grip

In this grip, the right hand stick **(the opposite if you're left handed)** is held with the thumb and index finger just behind the lettering which appears on it. Think of a pin going through the thumb, stick, and index finger in a straight line and the stick pivoting at that point. The other fingers **all** gently rest **on** the stick and follow the motion of the drumstick. With the traditional grip the right hand moves from the wrist in an up and down motion.

With the left hand, the stick is held at the point where the thumb and index finger join the hand. The top two fingers (index and middle) rest over the top of the stick while the remaining two fingers are under the stick. The thumb is positioned over the stick and gently rests on the index finger. With the traditional grip the left wrist moves much the same as when you turn a doorknob.

Photo by Ruya Qian

The Matched Grip

The other popular grip is the matched grip. With this grip, both hands are held like the right hand grip (described in the traditional grip copy). There are two distinct advantages to the matched grip: (1) both hands are held exactly the same and require only one wrist motion; (2) many drummers find it easier to maneuver around the drumset.

Photo by Hélène Dallaire

Try both grips. Choose the one that seems to fit you the best.

STARTING TO PLAY

Sit comfortably at the drumset. Hold your sticks in the matched grip or traditional grip position. Then let your arms drop to your sides with the sticks resting loosely in your hands. Next, bring your arms up from the elbow so that they are at a 90° angle to your body and are parallel to the floor. This is the proper playing position for the drumset. Notice that your shoulders and upper arms are in a completely relaxed position.

The first drum that you'll play on is the snare drum.

The top head of the snare drum is called the batter head. The bottom head is called the snare head. The tensioning procedure is the same as the bass drum. In order to arrive at a clean, clear snare drum sound, both heads should be tensioned tightly. The snares should contact the snare head evenly without being too loose. Snares that do not contact the head properly may result in unwanted buzzing of the snare drum when the other drums are being played.

Batter Head

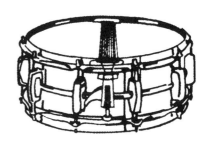

Snare Head

Exercise for the Hands

 Ex. 1   Play four taps on the snare drum with the right hand.

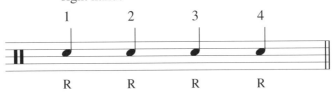

 Ex. 2   Play four taps on the snare drum with the left hand.

8

Ex. 3 Play four taps on the snare drum with each hand. Do this several times.

NOTE: If a deeper sound is required from the snare drum, leave the bottom head tensioned tightly but loosen the top head about 10 to 20 percent. While tuning, keep in mind that the head tension should be approximately the same at every tension screw.

Exercise for the Feet

The next drum you'll play on is the bass drum.

 Ex. 1 Play eight even strokes on the bass drum (use your right foot on the bass pedal). Do this several times.

The first cymbal we'll use is the hi-hat cymbal.

 Ex. 1 The hi-hat cymbals are the two cymbals that are clamped to the hi-hat stand. Place your left foot on the pedal at the base of the hi-hat stand, and play eight even beats with the hi-hat.

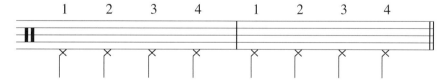

 Ex. 2 Now, repeat the bass drum beats. Along with it, play the hi-hat on every other beat. Do this several times.

SOME BASIC ELEMENTS 🔊

The Staff

Music is written on a structure called a staff. The staff consists of five horizontal lines and the four spaces between these lines. On melodic instruments, each line or space represents a specific pitch. Since drums do not normally play specific pitches, the various staff positions are used to represent different drums and cymbals. For example, the snare drum is represented by notes placed in the third space, the bass drum by notes written in the first space, the hi-hat cymbal by x's written directly below the first line.

As new drums or cymbals are introduced, a new staff position will be used to show you the pattern that must be played on that drum or cymbal.

Time Values

Divisions of time in music are called beats. The physical appearance of a note tells exactly how many beats it receives. The following illustration shows the most common types of notes and their time values.

Whole Note	**Half Note**	**Quarter Note**
4 beats	2 beats	1 beat

Rests

Rests are symbols used in music to indicate a period of silence. The physical appearance of a rest determines how long the period of silence will be. The following illustration shows the most common rests and their corresponding time values.

Whole Rest	**Half Rest**	**Quarter Rest**
4 beats of silence	2 beats of silence	1 beat of silence

Bar Lines and Measures

Each staff is divided into sections by vertical lines called bar lines. The sections between bar lines are called measures. A double bar line (‖) indicates the end of a song.

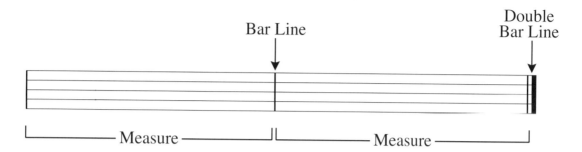

The 4/4 Time Signature

From now on, at the beginning of each exercise or rhythm pattern in this book, there will be a set of two numbers called the time signature. While there are many different time signatures, the one used in this book is 4/4. The upper number tells how many beats there are in each measure, and the bottom number tells what kind of note receives one beat.

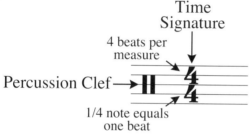

Counting and the Single Stroke

The single stroke (or single stroke roll as it is sometimes referred to) is the rapid succession of single beats performed by alternating the hands so that the drumsticks strike the drum evenly from one stick to another. Your hands should move from the wrists only, and the sticks should be held comfortably. It is important not to hold the stick too tightly so that the natural rebound of the drumstick can be utilized. To help you acquire speed and control of this important fundamental rudiment, exaggerate the motion of the wrists in order to follow the rebounding stick.

Repeat Signs

Repeat signs are used to indicate that a certain section of music is to be played again. Most often, repeat signs appear in sets of two. There is a repeat sign (‖:) at the beginning of a section to be repeated and another repeat sign (:‖) at the end of a section. When two repeat signs are present, play to the second repeat sign and then return to the first repeat sign and play the entire section once more.

NOTE: On the accompanying audio, the example is played only once through.

Ex. 1   Count quarter notes while playing the single stroke on the snare drum (or practice pad).

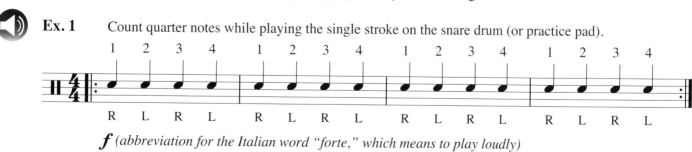

f (abbreviation for the Italian word "forte," which means to play loudly)

Eighth Notes

When a quarter note is divided in half, a new type of note called the eighth note is formed. Eighth notes are played twice as fast as quarter notes. Each eighth note (♪) or eighth rest (𝄾) is worth half of a beat. Because it takes two eighth notes to equal one quarter, it is then possible to have eight eighth notes in each bar.

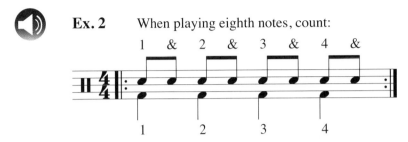

Ex. 2   When playing eighth notes, count:

A Single Stroke Exercise

The purpose of the following exercise is the development of control and speed of the single stroke. Begin the exercise slowly and gradually. Increase the speed of the hands until you're playing as fast as possible. Maintain the fastest speed for a few seconds, then reverse the procedure by **gradually** slowing down until you are back to the original tempo. Be sure to rotate your hands with a maximum wrist turn in accordance with the natural rebound of the drumstick.

Ex. 3 In the following exercise, the notes show **slow to fast to slow** only and should not be interpreted exactly as written.

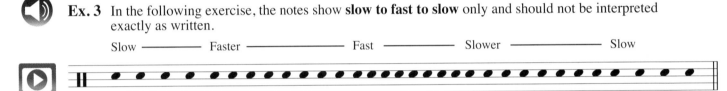

Notice that as the strokes get faster, the rebounds are closer to the drum head.

Basic Pattern

The following is a basic drumset pattern in quarter notes. The x's marked directly on the top line of the staff indicate the part played on the ride cymbal (for location of the ride cymbal, see page 3).

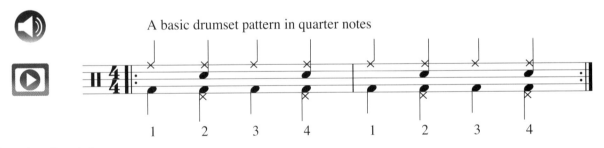

A basic drumset pattern in quarter notes

Exercise Breakdown

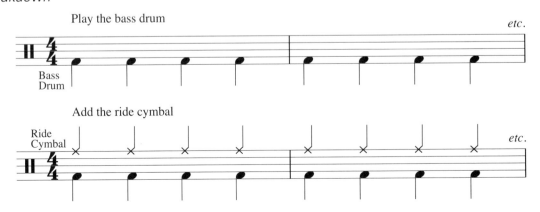

Play the bass drum

etc.

Add the ride cymbal

etc.

Add the hi-hat on counts 2 and 4

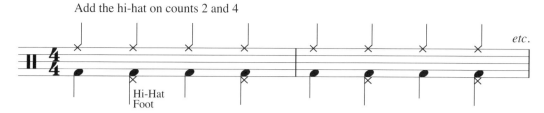

Hi-Hat
Foot

Complete the pattern by adding the snare drum on counts 2 and 4 along with the hi-hat

Snare
Drum

Quarters and Eighths

In order to play and read at the drumset, it is important that you know how to stop and start the hands while the feet continue playing. Begin the following exercise on the bass drum by playing steady quarter notes in 4/4 time. Then add the hi-hat on 2 & 4 as indicated by the x notehead. After you have started your feet playing in a comfortable 4/4 pattern, proceed to play the exercise. Alternate the right and left hands on the snare drum. Remember to keep the feet going, but do not play the snare drum on the rests.

Ex. 1 Counting and playing quarter notes

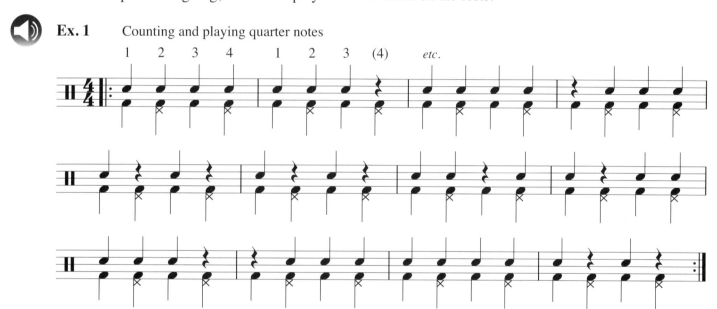

Ex. 2 Counting and playing eighth notes

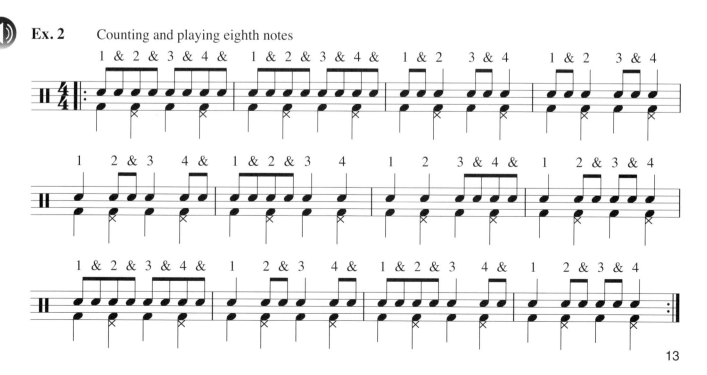

PLAYING AROUND THE SET

The following exercise uses three tom-toms. The notes written in the fourth space of the staff indicate the beats that must be played on rack tom #1. The notes written on the fourth line indicate the beats that must be played on rack tom #2. The notes written in the second space indicate the beats that must be played on the floor tom.

NOTE: The "x" notehead written above the staff on the ledger line indicates the crash cymbal.

Quarter Notes and Eighth Notes Around the Set

 Ex. 1* Play the quarter notes on the snare drum and tom-toms as written. Start each of the following exercises slowly. As the exercises become more familiar, increase the tempo.

*This exercise is designed for the basic five piece drumset (two rack toms). If you have the four piece set (one rack tom), double the rack tom drum part on the one drum. If you have more than the basic five piece setup, choose the toms that will accommodate the exercise.

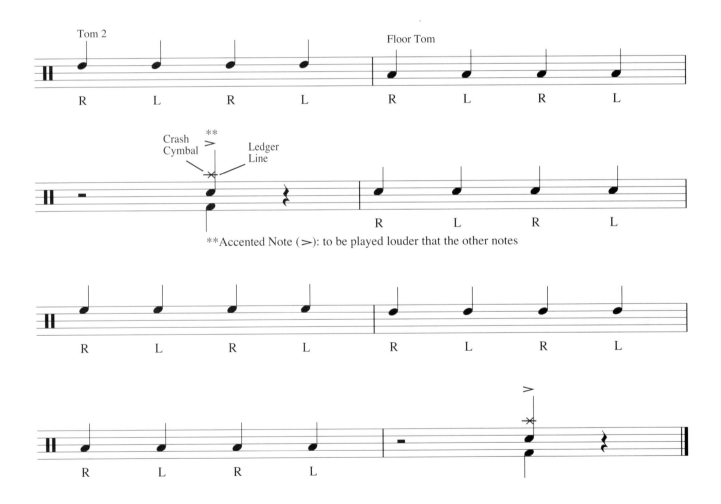

**Accented Note (>): to be played louder that the other notes

Ex. 2 Now add the bass drum and hi-hat

 Ex. 3 Play eighth notes around the set as written

Ex. 4 Now add the bass drum and hi-hat to the eighth note exercise

EIGHT NOTE PATTERNS ON THE DRUMSET

In this lesson you'll learn some modern eighth note patterns that can be applied to most eighth note based music. You will also learn to use independent bass drum technique against the basic pulse of the snare drum and ride cymbal pattern. You should practice playing the ride cymbal pattern both on the ride cymbal and on the closed hi-hat. When playing on the ride cymbal, the hi-hat closes as usual on 2 and 4. However, when playing on the closed hi-hat, keep the hi-hat cymbals closed tightly together throughout.

Rock Pattern in 4/4 time

Ex. 1

Exercise Breakdown

Play the bass drum

Add the hi-hat on counts 2 and 4

Add the ride cymbal in eighths (two eighths to every one quarter)

Add the snare drum along with the hi-hat on counts 2 and 4

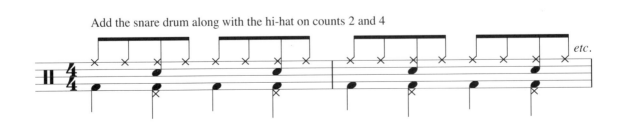

'50s Style Rock Pattern

Ex. 2

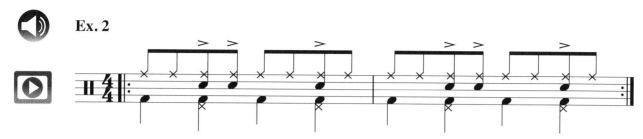

Exercise Breakdown

Play the ride cymbal in even eighths

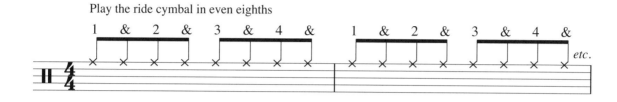

Add the hi-hat on counts 2 and 4

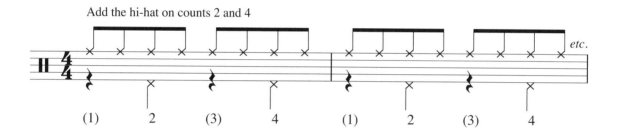

Add the bass drum on all 4 counts

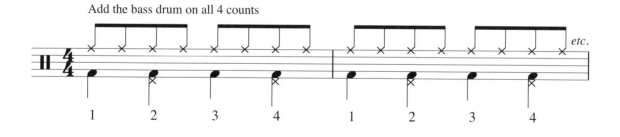

Add the snare drum part (accent the snare drum but not the cymbals)

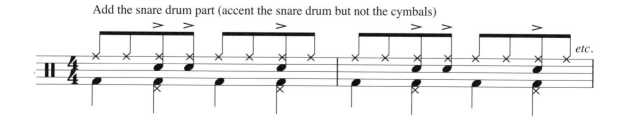

Basic Rock Pattern with the Bass Drum in Eighth Notes

Ex. 3

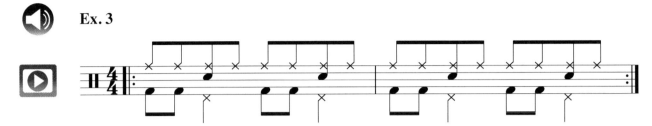

Exercise Breakdown

Play the ride cymbal in even eighths

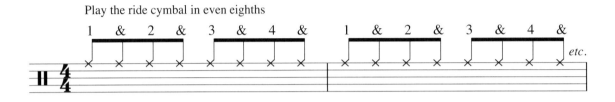

Add the hi-hat on counts 2 and 4

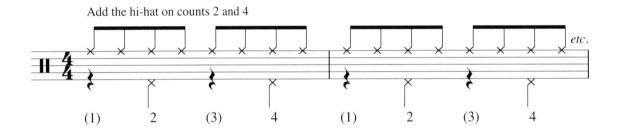

Add the bass drum part

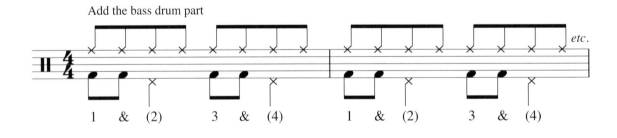

Add the snare drum on counts 2 and 4

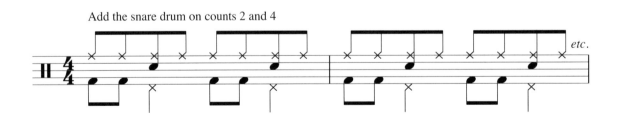

Motown Rhythm and Blues Beat

Ex. 4

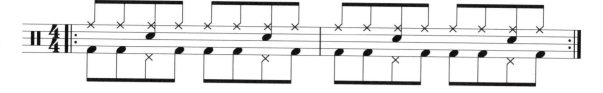

Exercise Breakdown

Play the ride cymbal in even eighths

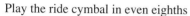

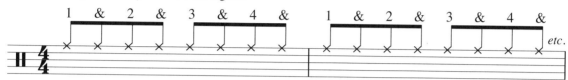

Add the hi-hat on counts 2 and 4

Add the bass drum part

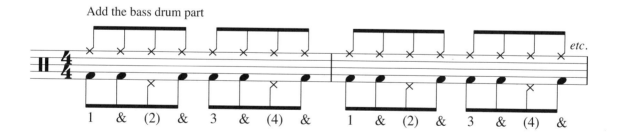

Add the snare drum on counts 2 and 4

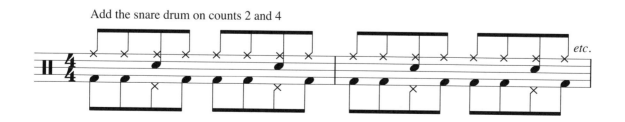

Disco Beat

 Ex. 5 Notice that both the bass drum and the hi-hat play on all four beats of the bar. The hi-hat ride beat is therefore a series of open (o) and closed eighth notes. This happens automatically when you play the eighths on the hi-hat as it opens and closes on the four quarter notes of the bar.

Ride on the hi-hat only

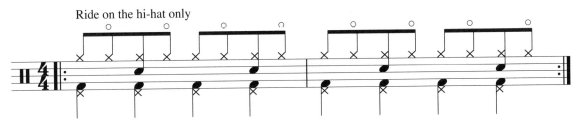

Exercise Breakdown

Play on the closed hi-hat in even eighths

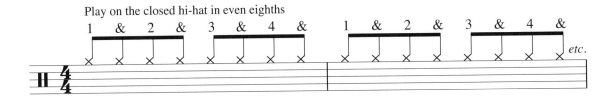

With the hi-hat foot play quarter notes (continue the ride)

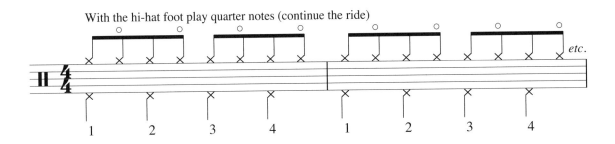

Add the bass drum

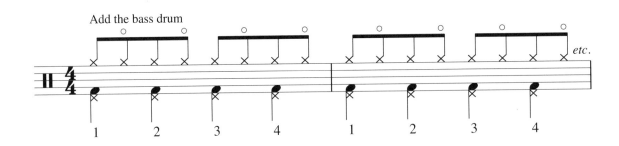

Add the snare drum on counts 2 and 4

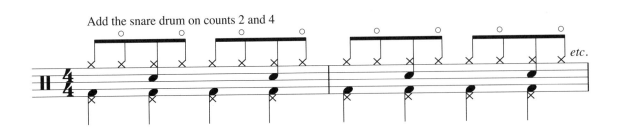

Bass Drum on the Upbeats

Ex. 6

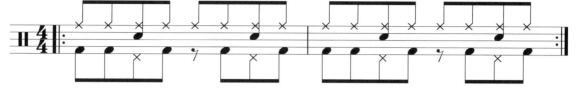

Exercise Breakdown

Play the ride cymbal in even eighths

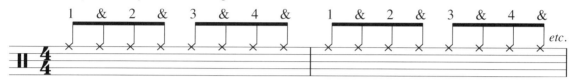

Add the hi-hat on counts 2 and 4

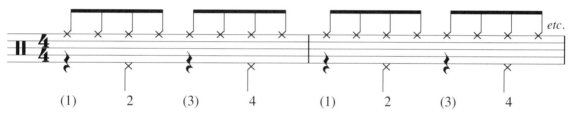

Add the bass drum part

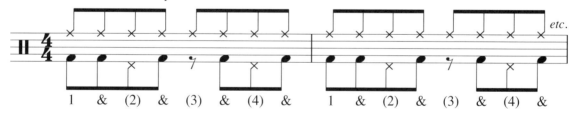

Add the snare drum on counts 2 and 4

Improvise

Ex. 7   Improvise your own bass drum eighth note patterns against the ride cymbal, hi-hat, and snare drum.

Playing a Drum Fill

A drum fill is a short drum solo used to add excitement to the band. Drum fills may be written out or improvised for a predetermined number of bars.

Ex. 8a   Play the basic rock pattern for two bars. Go from bar 2 to bar 3 without stopping the time and play the drum fill around the drumset in single strokes in bars 3, 4, 5, and 6. Notice the bass drum changes to quarter notes during the drum fill. After playing the written rock pattern, play the other previously learned patterns with this drum fill exercise.

Ex. 8b   Here is a two-bar fill as an option.

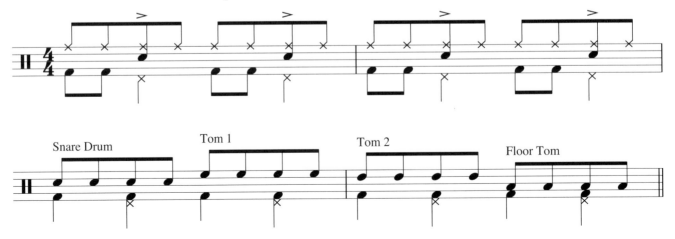

THE DOUBLE STROKE ROLL
Bounce Strokes
Example

R R L L R R L L R R L L R R L L R R

Many professionals feel that the two most fundamental rudiments required for drumset playing are the single stroke and double stroke. Most of the other drum rudiments are combinations of these two.

When you begin playing the double stroke, start slowly by making two distinct taps with each hand. As you play faster, the second tap changes to a stick bounce. In order to do this, you strike the drum head once and then allow the natural rebound of the drumstick to make the second tap automatically. It's important to learn to control the natural rebound (bounce) of the drumstick.

The Double Stroke—Slow to Fast to Slow

 Ex. 1 Start slowly and gradually increase the speed of the double stroke until the sticks are rebounding comfortably in the hands; then, gradually return to the original tempo.

Slow —————— Faster ———————— Fast ———— Slower ———————— Slow

R R L L R R L L R R L L R R L L R R L L R R L L R R L L R R L L R R L L

No bounce ————————————————— To bounce ———— No bounce

The Open Roll

The roll is the drummer's way of sustaining sound from the drum. The open roll is the double stroke played at a fast steady tempo. The important thing to remember about the open roll is that the drumsticks never play more than two taps in each hand, no matter how fast the roll is played.

Fast and steady

R R L L R R L L   R R L L R R L L   R R L L R R L L   R R L L R R L L

Example

The notation in this example tells you that each whole note is rolled for the entire four count duration of each bar. The rhythm of the double strokes should be as fast as it takes to keep the roll tight. In other words, the basic tempo of the quarter note does not dictate the speed of the hands.

Rolls as notated in drum music look like this:

1   2   3   4   1   2   3   4   1   2   3   4

SIXTEENTH NOTES

Counting and Playing Sixteenths

Sixteenth notes are the equivalent of the quarter note divided into four equal parts. Therefore, each sixteenth note gets 1/4 of a count.

Example

Sixteenth notes are counted as follows:

1 e & a 2 e & a 3 e & a 4 e & a

Ex. 1   Count and play sixteenths on the snare drum.

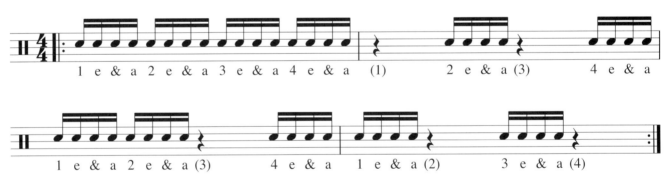

Ex. 2   Play the same exercise with the bass drum and hi-hat included.

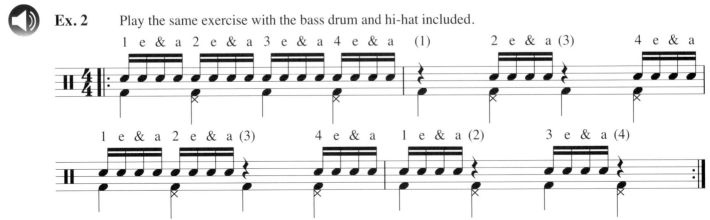

Sixteenths and the Drumset

Ex. 1   Play double strokes in sixteenth notes on the snare drum.

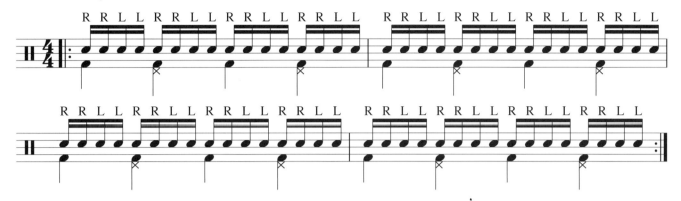

Ex. 2   Play the following exercise around the set.

Ex. 3   Play the following exercise with single strokes.

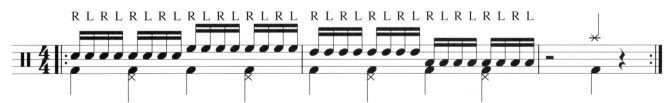

Improvising with Sixteenths (using single and double strokes)

 Ex. 1   Singles and doubles on the snare drum

 Ex. 2   After mastering the preceding on the snare drum, play the same exercise around the drumset.

Ex. 3   Improvise with double strokes in sixteenth notes around the set. Include the bass drum and hi-hat.

Keep the sixteenths flowing smoothly as you move from one drum to another.

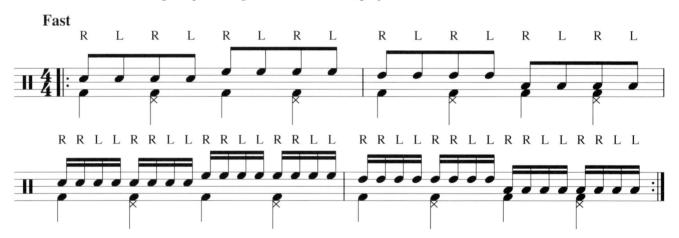

Ex. 4   Improvise with single strokes in sixteenth notes around the set. Include the bass drum and hi-hat.

Eighth and Sixteenth Combination Strokes on the Snare Drum

Ex. 1   Play on the snare drum only with alternate sticking.

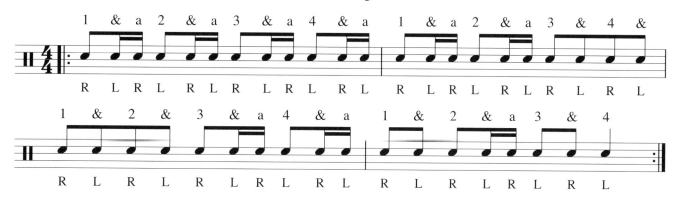

Ex. 2   The previous exercise with the bass drum and hi-hat included

Ex. 3   Play on the snare drum only with alternate sticking.

Ex. 4   The previous exercise with the bass drum and hi-hat included

Ex. 5   Play on the snare drum only with alternate sticking.

 Ex. 6   The previous exercise with the bass drum and hi-hat included.

EIGHTH AND SIXTEENTH NOTE ROCK PATTERNS ▶

Funk Pattern with Sixteenth Notes on the Bass Drum

 Ex. 1   Eighths and sixteenths with the bass drum against the eighth note ride

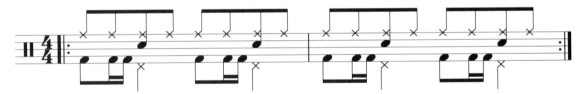

Exercise Breakdown

Play the ride cymbal in even eighths

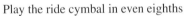

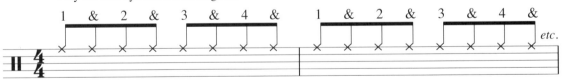

Add the hi-hat on counts 2 and 4

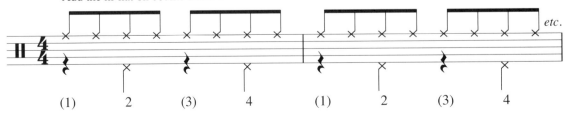

Add the bass drum part

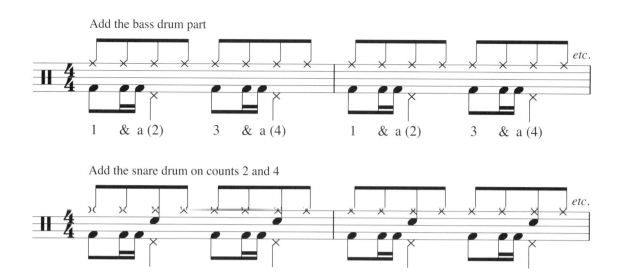

1 & a (2)   3 & a (4)   1 & a (2)   3 & a (4)

Add the snare drum on counts 2 and 4

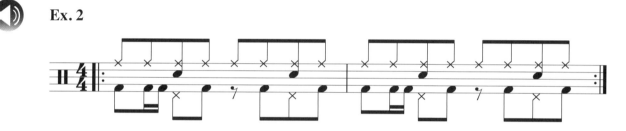

Funk Pattern with Eighth Note Upbeats on the Bass Drum

Ex. 2

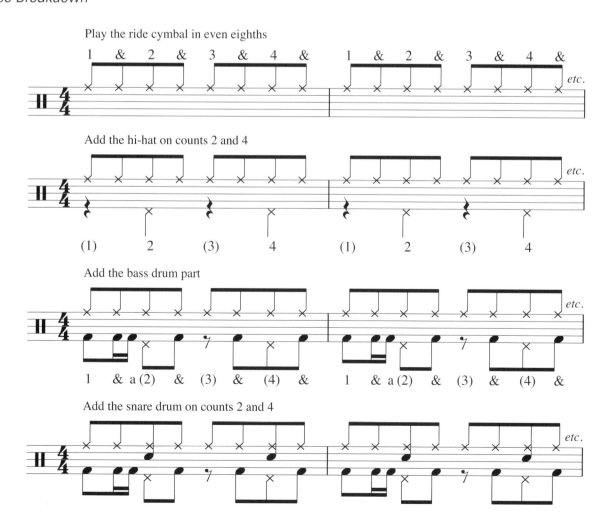

Exercise Breakdown

Play the ride cymbal in even eighths

1 & 2 & 3 & 4 &   1 & 2 & 3 & 4 &   etc.

Add the hi-hat on counts 2 and 4

etc.

(1)   2   (3)   4   (1)   2   (3)   4

Add the bass drum part

etc.

1 & a (2) & (3) & (4) &   1 & a (2) & (3) & (4) &

Add the snare drum on counts 2 and 4

etc.

Urban Beat with Sixteenth Note Pattern on the Bass Drum

 Ex. 3

*A dot adds half the value to the note or rest that precedes it. Therefore, the note in this example is the value of two sixteenths ( ) and the dot adds one more sixteenth ( ), resulting in a dotted eighth note ( ).

Exercise Breakdown

Play the ride cymbal in even eighths

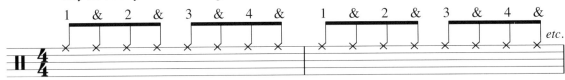

Add the hi-hat on counts 2 and 4

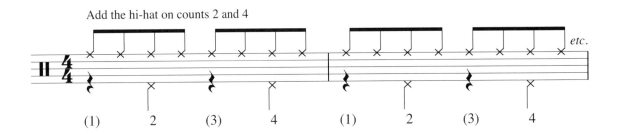

Add the bass drum part

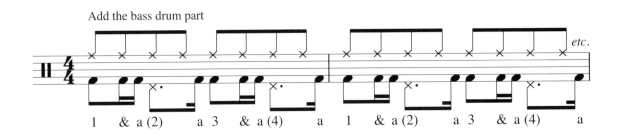

Add the snare drum on counts 2 and 4

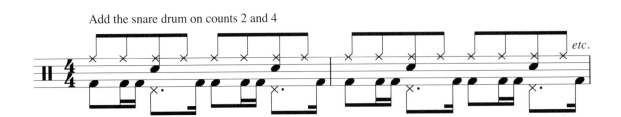

Rap Beat with Sixteenth Note Pattern on the Bass Drum

Ex. 4

Not too fast

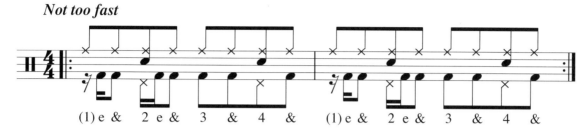

Exercise Breakdown

Play the ride cymbal in even eighths

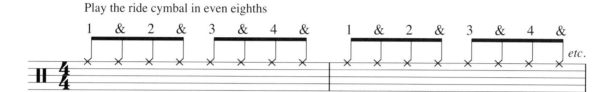

Add the hi-hat on counts 2 and 4

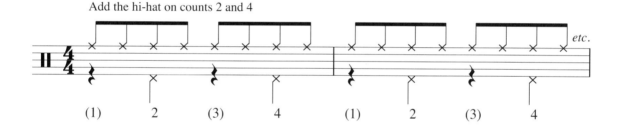

Add the bass drum part

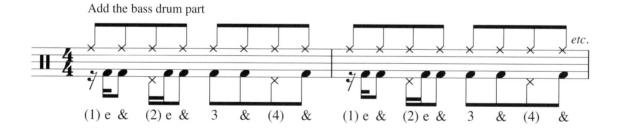

Add the snare drum on counts 2 and 4

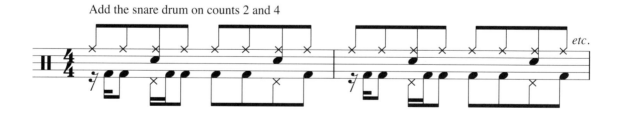

Ex. 5 Improvise your own bass drum patterns against the ride cymbal. The hi-hat may play on beats 2 and 4 or all beats. The snare should continue on the 2 and 4 "backbeat" pattern.

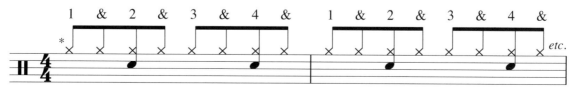

*The ride cymbal part may also be played on the closed hi-hat.

Ex. 6   Play sixteenth notes on the ride cymbal or closed hi-hat and repeat Exercises 1 through 4 on pages 28 through 31.

When playing with both hands on the closed hi-hat at faster tempos, use this sticking.

Drum Fill in Sixteenth Notes

Ex. 7a   Play and learn the exercise with the rock pattern that's written. Play the drum fill using both single strokes and double strokes. Experiment by substituting some of the other rock patterns in the first two bars of this exercise.

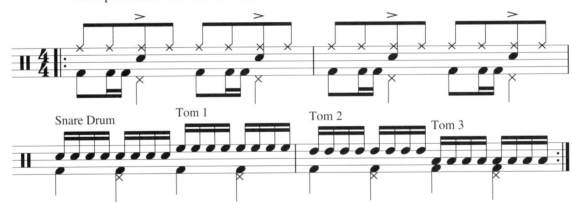

Ex. 7b   Try the one-bar fill as well.

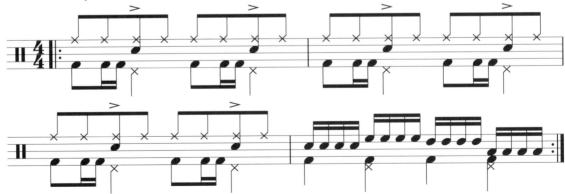

Ex. 8   Repeat the drum fill exercise. However, this time use sixteenths on the ride cymbal. Play the drum fill as you did in Exercise 7a.

THE TRIPLET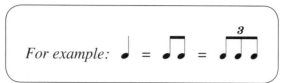

A triplet is a group of three notes (indicated on the music by a number "3") played in the same amount of time ordinarily given to two notes of the same time value.

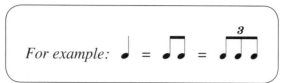

The eighth note triplet divides the quarter note into three equal parts.

Ex. 1 Count and play triplets in 4/4 time on the snare drum.

Ex. 2 Add the bass drum and hi-hat to the preceding exercise.

Ex. 3 Count and play triplets around the set.

Ex. 4 Add the bass drum and hi-hat to the preceding exercise.

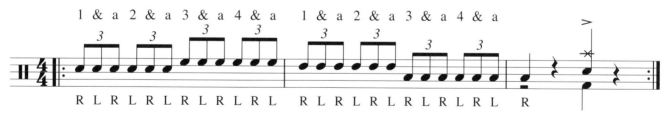

Ex. 5 Improvise around the set with triplets using single strokes only. Keep a steady beat with the bass drum and hi-hat.

THE RIDE CYMBAL AND JAZZ (SWING)

The ride cymbal carries one of the most important functions of the drumset. That function is playing "the time" (keeping the beat), and establishing the rhythmic feel of the piece being played. The ride cymbal is the heart of the rhythm section. (The rhythm section in a band includes: drums, bass, keyboard, percussion, and guitar.)

Earlier you played a basic rock pattern. Now you'll learn the basic jazz ride cymbal pattern.

The ride cymbal pattern comes from the triplet rhythm:

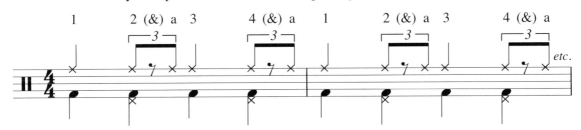

This pattern may also be shown as follows:

The words "play today" fit the rhythm of the jazz ride cymbal pattern.

The ride cymbal is played with one hand only — the right hand for right handed drummers and the left hand for left handed drummers.

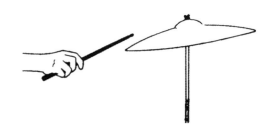

The cymbal should be played with the bead (or tip) of the stick near the edge of the cymbal.

Basic Drumset Jazz Swing Pattern in 4/4 Time

Ex. 1

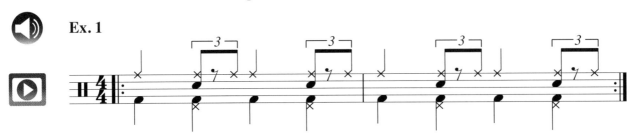

34

Exercise Breakdown

Play the ride cymbal

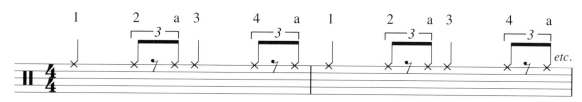

Add the hi-hat on counts 2 and 4

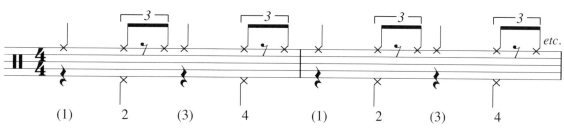

Add the bass drum

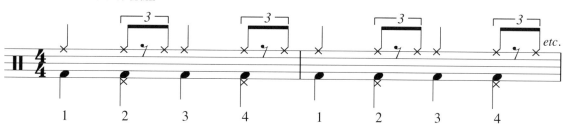

Add the snare drum along with the hi-hat on counts 2 and 4

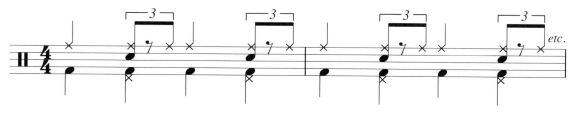

The jazz ride beat works with many styles of music including jazz, folk, country, swing, bluegrass, and dixieland. Find some recordings that include one of these categories and listen for the ride cymbal. Headphones work best for hearing music to play along with.

The Shuffle Rhythm

Ex. 2   The shuffle rhythm is the forerunner of the jazz ride cymbal beat and still is the basic rhythmic pattern for many blues compositions. It, too, is based on the triplet rhythm.

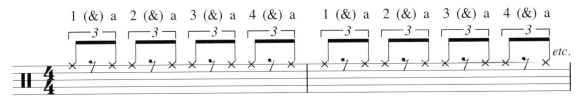

This pattern may also be shown as follows:

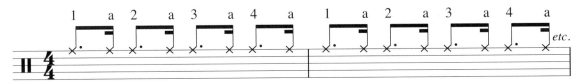

"Kansas City" Shuffle

 Ex. 3

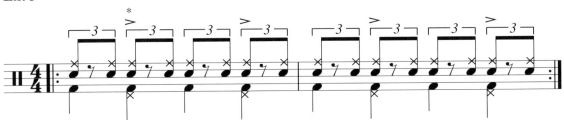

*When playing this shuffle beat, the ride cymbal and the snare drum are both accented.

Exercise Breakdown

Play the ride cymbal

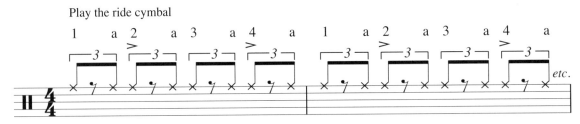

Add the bass drum and hi-hat

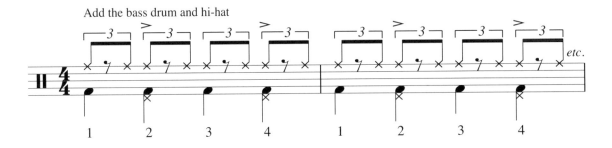

Add the snare drum along with the ride cymbal with an accent on counts 2 and 4

INDEPENDENCE AND THE RIDE CYMBAL

The term "independence" refers to the technique of playing patterns on the snare drum that complement the music while the ride cymbal continues its pattern uninterrupted.

The Jazz Ride Cymbal Pattern and the Shuffle Rhythm Played at the Same Time

Ex. 1

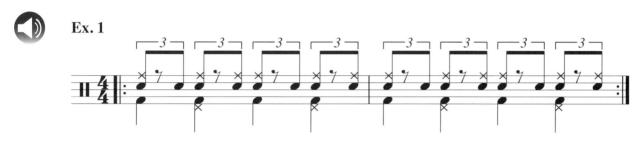

Exercise Breakdown

Play the ride cymbal

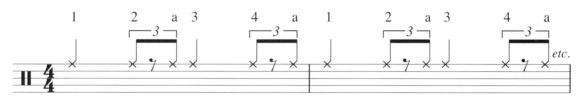

Add the bass drum and hi-hat

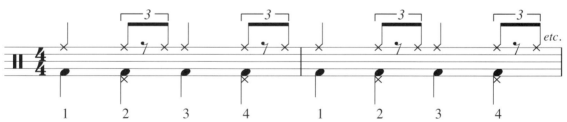

Add the shuffle rhythm on the snare drum

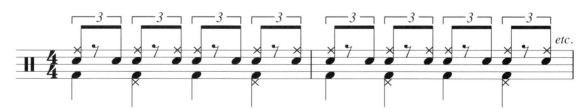

37

Jazz Ride Cymbal Pattern and Triplets Played at the Same Time

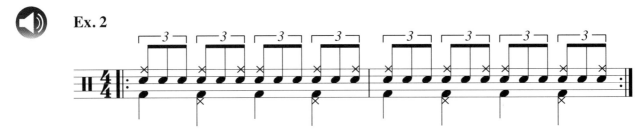

Ex. 2

Exercise Breakdown

Play the ride cymbal

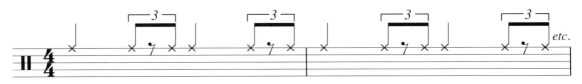

Add the bass drum and hi-hat

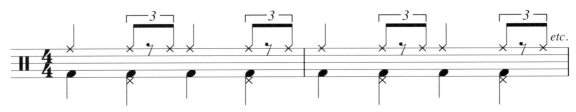

Add the snare drum in triplets

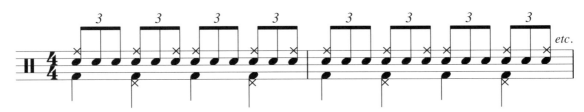

Mixed Patterns

Ex. 3

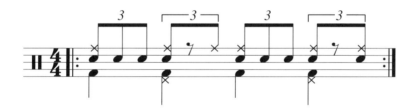

There are endless combinations of patterns that may be played against the jazz cymbal ride. Eventually you will learn to play patterns with hands and feet independently, adding punctuation to the overall rhythmic feel.

Ex. 4   Improvise your own independent patterns against the jazz cymbal ride pattern. Keep the ride cymbal and patterns musical and flowing.

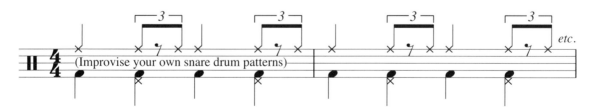

Country "Two Beat" Swing Pattern

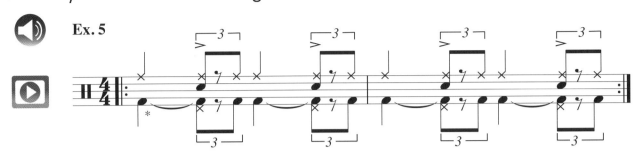

Ex. 5

*A tie is a curved line which connects notes on the same line or space of the staff. The value of the second note is added to the first note. The tied note is counted but **not** played.

Exercise Breakdown

Play the ride cymbal

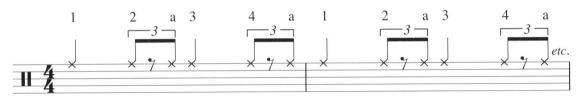

Add the hi-hat on counts 2 and 4

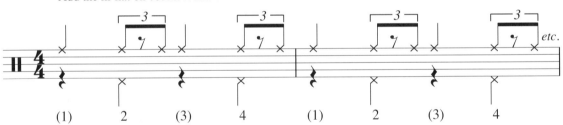

Add the bass drum

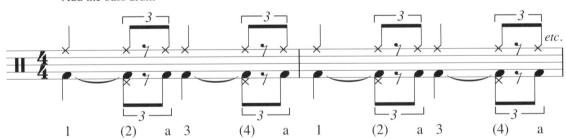

Add the snare drum on counts 2 and 4

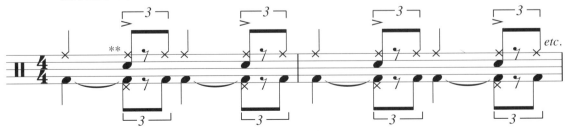

**Only the snare drum should be accented.

Nashville Country Rock

Ex. 6

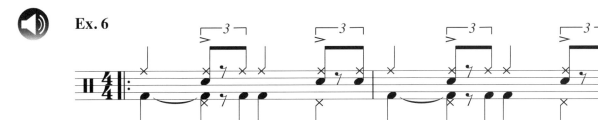

Exercise Breakdown

Play the ride cymbal

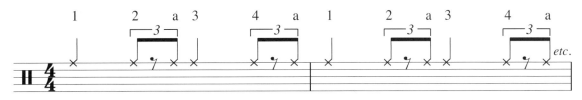

Add the hi-hat on counts 2 and 4

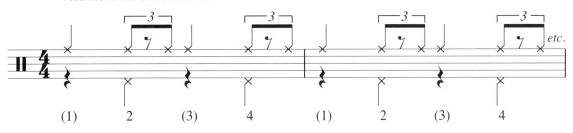

Add the bass drum

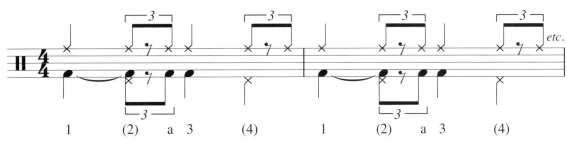

Add the snare drum

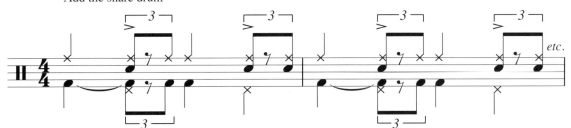

Drum Fill in Triplets

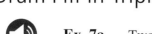

Ex. 7a   Two-Bar Fill

Ex. 7b   One-Bar Fill

Slow Blues Beat

Ex. 8   The next pattern has a metronome marking of ♩ = 60 written at the beginning of the music. The metronome is a device which helps to keep time by making a click sound a specified number of times per minute. This particular mark means that the metronome should be set at 60 and each click represents the length of a quarter note. Metronome marks indicate tempo. If at first you cannot play the pattern at this tempo, practice it slower and gradually increase the speed as it becomes more comfortable.

♩ = 60

Exercise Breakdown

Play the ride cymbal

1 & a 2 & a 3 & a 4 & a   1 & a 2 & a 3 & a 4 & a

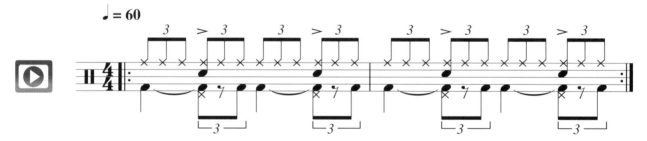

Add the hi-hat on counts 2 and 4

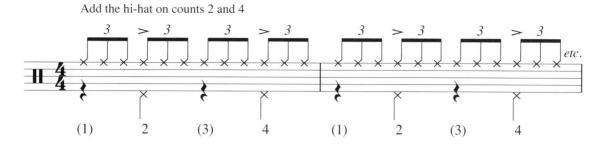

Add the bass drum

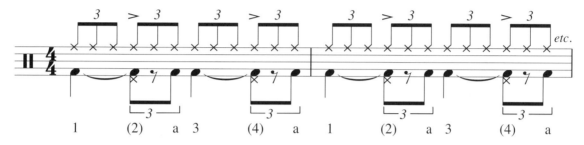

Add the snare drum on counts 2 and 4

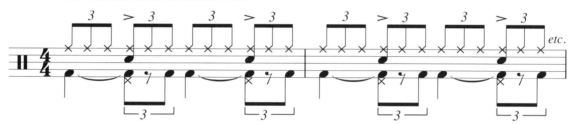

Slow Blues Beat with a Sixteenth Note Fill

Ex. 9a   One-Bar Fill w/ sixteenths

♩ = 72

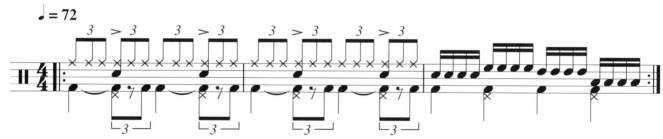

Ex. 9b   One-Bar Fill w/ sextuplets

♩ = 72

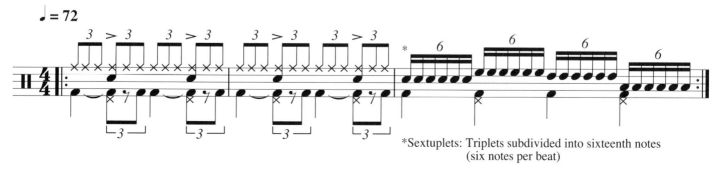

*Sextuplets: Triplets subdivided into sixteenth notes
(six notes per beat)

VALUABLE SNARE DRUM RUDIMENTS

The Flam

The flam beat requires concentration and dexterity in order to be played well. The flam is comprised of a main note preceded by a grace note. The grace note is played close to the main note and is considered part of the same beat.

Example:

 Ex. 1

The grace note indicates that the drum is struck first and the main note indicates that the drum is struck immediately after the grace note. The hand playing the grace note will always be closer to the drum head. When one flam is played, the hands then reverse so the hand that played the main note will now play the grace note. Always aim to keep the grace note hand still and close to the drum while you are switching hands for the next flam.

Right-Handed Flam

Left-Handed Flam

The Closed Roll or Buzz Roll

The closed roll, often referred to as the buzz or press roll, is a series of buzz sounds from each alternating stick. To begin developing the buzz roll, play a short relaxed buzz with each stick. After you can play a clear buzz in each hand, increase the speed until the buzz connects into one continuous sound.

 Ex. 2a

R L R L R L R L R L R L R Closed Roll

p (soft)

In order to play the buzz roll louder, you must apply more pressure to the drumstick and at the same time increase the speed of the alternating hands.

Ex. 2b Practice playing the buzz roll from soft to loud to soft. Take your time.

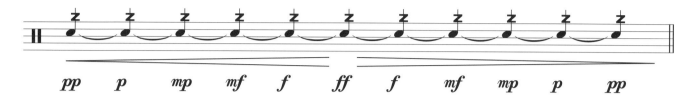

The dynamic markings translate as follows:

pp —pianissimo, very soft
p —piano, soft
mp —mezzo piano, medium soft

mf —mezzo forte, medium loud
f —forte, loud
ff —fortissimo, very loud

The Five Stroke Roll

The five stroke roll may be played both open and closed and is comprised of three hand motions. The first two hand motions are bounce strokes while the third hand motion is a single tap. The five stroke roll alternates from hand to hand.

Exercise Breakdown

 Ex. 3   The open five stroke roll

The closed five stroke roll

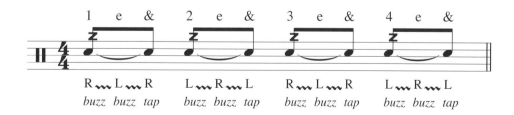

Eighth notes and the five stroke roll (bass drum and hi-hat included)

The Paradiddle

Singles and doubles are the two most important basic techniques for this method. Once you feel comfortable with your single and double technique, proceed to the rudiment that combines both: the paradiddle.

To develop the paradiddle to a smooth fast tempo, play the natural accent that falls on the first beat of each paradiddle. The double strokes should be bounced in order to attain maximum speed.

Improvising Exercise

 Ex. 2   Improvise in sixteenth note paradiddles around the drumset. The bass drum should be played on all four counts and the hi-hat on counts 2 and 4. Start the paradiddles on the snare drum. Then gradually work your way out and around all the drums of your set until you're improvising a paradiddle drum solo.

Review

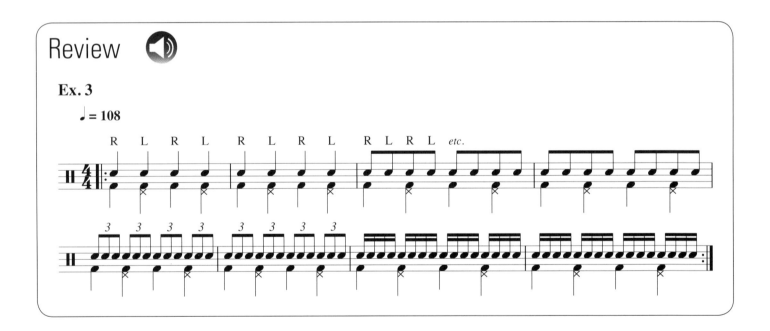

USING THE HI-HAT CYMBALS

Controlling the placement of the open hi-hat sound is one of the most subtle challenges of the recording studio drummer. Here are some progressive beats that utilize the open and closed sound of the hi-hat along with syncopated patterns on the bass drum.

After learning these patterns, it is suggested that you continue by creating your own.

    ○ =   Open sound (otherwise the hi-hat cymbals remain closed; i.e., only open on the ○).

    ○ − =   Open hi-hat over two sixteenth notes.

NOTE: When playing the open hi-hat sound, the preferred "open" sound is produced when the hi-hat cymbals are lightly touching one another.

In Eighth Notes

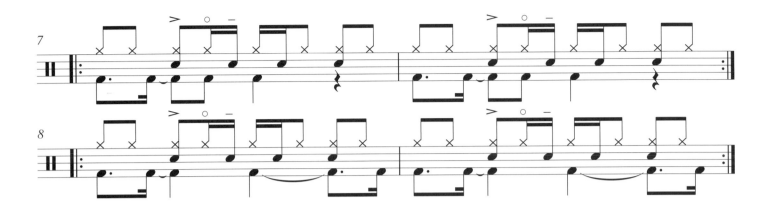

In Sixteenth Notes

Playing the hi-hat with both hands in sixteenth notes.

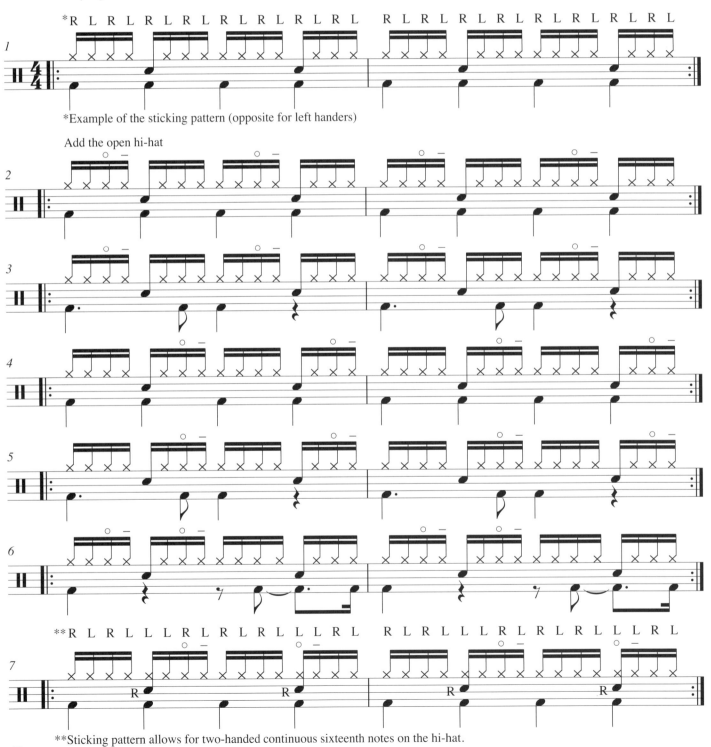

*Example of the sticking pattern (opposite for left handers)

Add the open hi-hat

**Sticking pattern allows for two-handed continuous sixteenth notes on the hi-hat.

SINGLES AND DOUBLES

This series of exercises, once mastered, can be used as a daily warm-up routine.

Single Stroke Exercise

 Ex. 1 As a review, begin this exercise slowly, and **gradually** increase the speed of the hands until you are playing as fast as possible. Maintain your maximum speed for a few seconds, then **gradually** slow down until you are back to the original slow tempo. In this way, all tempos are covered. Be sure to rotate the wrists with a maximum turn in accordance with the natural rebound of the drumstick.

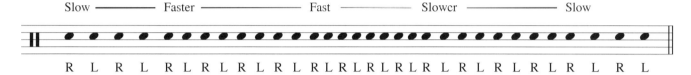

Repeat the Procedure with Double Strokes

 Ex. 2

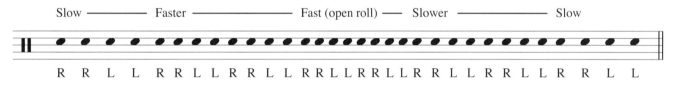

Changing Speed Exercise

 Ex. 3 Again, start slowly and gradually increase the speed. Because this exercise is **in tempo**, accompany the written notes with the bass drum and hi-hat. Play the bass drum on all four quarters and the hi-hat on 2 and 4.

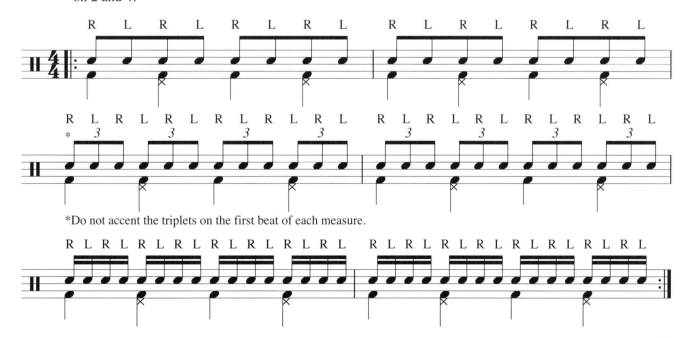

*Do not accent the triplets on the first beat of each measure.

Repeat the Preceding Exercise Using Double Strokes

 Ex. 4 Start slowly and gradually increase the tempo until maximum speed is attained. Then, gradually slow down to the original tempo.

*Triplets in doubles

 Ex. 5 Pick a comfortable, steady tempo and play Exercise 3 (singles) and Exercise 4 (doubles) around your drumset. Play the exercises as written, moving around your set as you choose.

Roll Exercise Without Changing the Motion of Your Hands

 Ex. 6 Play the single strokes with a consistent, relaxed, maximum wrist turn. When playing the double strokes, keep the wrist motion exactly the same and allow the drumstick to bounce on its own to make the double. Practice this exercise at a variety of tempos.

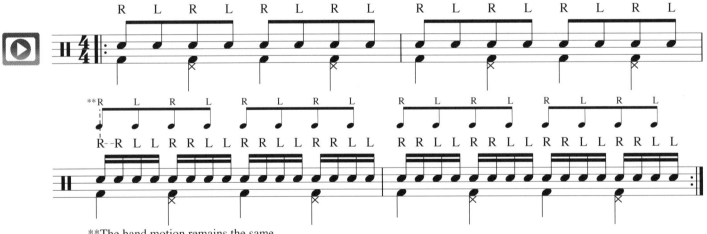

**The hand motion remains the same.

Three Stroke Bounce Exercise

 Ex. 7 A drumstick will bounce evenly three times. When you master the three bounce roll, you will have gained control and the feel of the maximum even drumstick bounce. Start slowly and gradually increase the tempo (without bass drum or hi-hat).

PLAYING TIME

The art of playing relaxed, comfortable time with the proper feel for the music being played is paramount to being a good drummer. Here are some exercises designed to develop a smooth, flowing cymbal ride in eighth notes. Play these exercises with an even, relaxed flow at a variety of steady tempos.

Four Rock Beats with an Eighth Note Cymbal Ride

Ex. 1

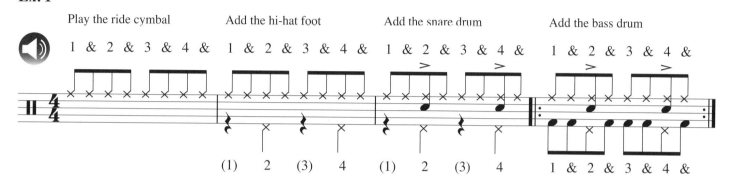

Ex. 2

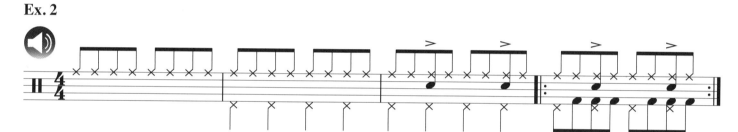

Ex. 3

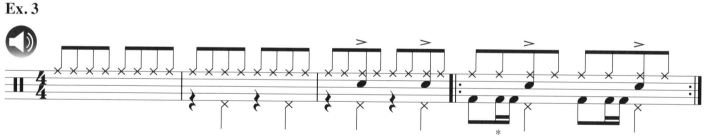

*Some drummers play the pedals up on their toes while others play with the foot flat. It's best to learn to play both ways: 1) up on the toes for power and, 2) with the flat foot for control.

Ex. 4

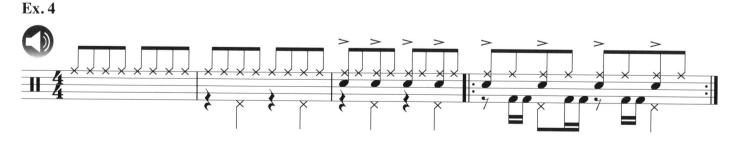

Occasionally check the accuracy of your time by playing these exercises and any others throughout this book with the aid of a metronome.

The Jazz Ride Beat

Although most of us are familiar with the sound of the jazz cymbal ride, it's important to understand and perfect its proper execution. Most jazz pros use a motion that combines the hand, arm, and shoulder. The motion of the cymbal ride might be compared to the delivery of a baseball pitch.

First, let's establish the rhythm of the jazz ride beat. This is the jazz cymbal ride written in triplets:

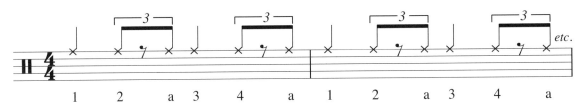

It's the most widely used jazz cymbal rhythm and is usually written as follows:

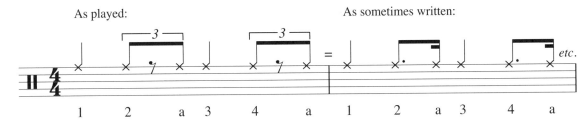

NOTE: Whether written in triplets or dotted eighths and sixteenths, the rhythm remains that of the triplet.

To play the cymbal ride, use the following motion:

- To begin, strike the first beat of the cymbal ride near the edge of the cymbal.

- Do the same for the second beat.

- After playing the second beat, raise the elbow straight (about 45°) out from the body, and play the skip beat and beat 3 of the cymbal ride

- Immediately after playing the third beat, let the elbow fall back to the side of your body. At the same time, bring the drumstick straight back behind the ear.

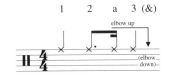

- On beat 4 and from then on, repeat the procedure.

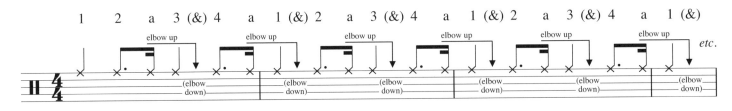

NOTE: While playing the jazz ride beat, the tip of the drumstick should stay relatively close to the same playing area on the cymbal.

When the tempo is slower, the motion is more exaggerated; as the tempo increases, the motion becomes less exaggerated. Once perfected, this cymbal ride motion improves most drummers' ability to play time with a consistent and even flow. This is particularly helpful in jazz drumming, where many times the other hand and bass drum are playing independently of the cymbal ride.*

Country Swing Beat

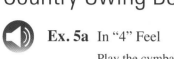

Ex. 5a In "4" Feel

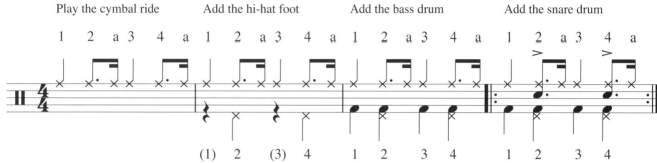

Ex. 5b In "2" Feel

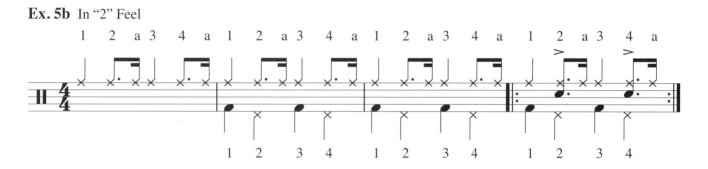

The Shuffle Rhythm Against the Jazz Cymbal Ride

Ex. 6

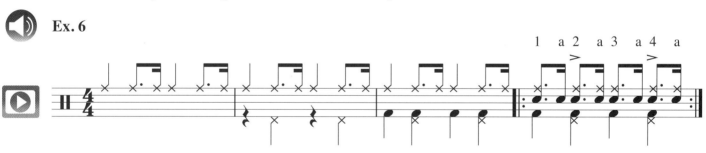

Triplets Against the Cymbal Ride

Ex. 7

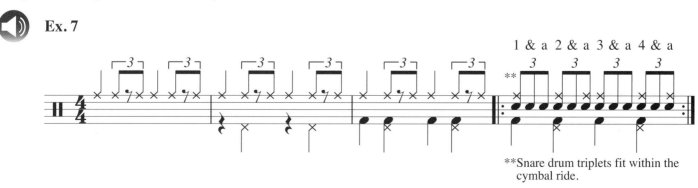

**Snare drum triplets fit within the cymbal ride.

*This is one way to play the ride cymbal; another would be with the elbow stationary at your side.

Changing the Cymbal Patterns Around

Ex. 8

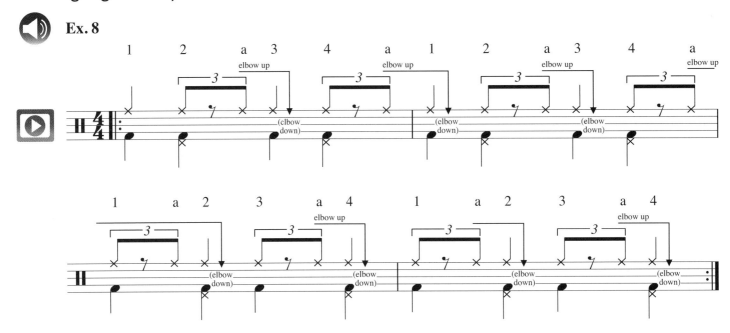

Three Cymbal Pattern in 4/4 Time

Ex. 9

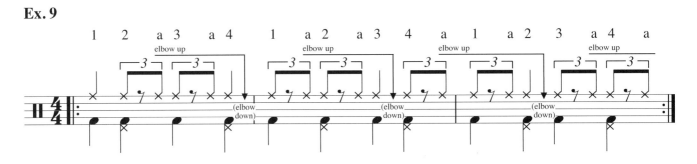

PLAYING ON THE HI-HAT

Now take some of the same ride cymbal patterns and apply them to the hi-hat cymbals. The symbol + represents the closed hi-hat, and the symbol ○ represents the open hi-hat. When the hi-hat is in the open position, just release the foot slightly so that the top cymbal is slightly touching the bottom cymbal. The symbol ⌀ indicates a position halfway between the open sound and the closed sound.

When playing on the hi-hat cymbals, the ride cymbal hand normally crosses over the hand playing on the snare drum (cross-handed). Some drummers have the ability to reverse the hands in order to avoid crossing over (open-handed). However, switching this way is not natural or practical for most drummers.

The "Two Beat" Hi-Hat Cymbal Ride

Ex. 10

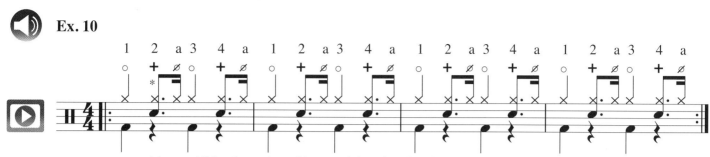

*As an additional exercise, add cross-stick on beat 2 and rack tom on beat 4 and 4 "a." (See page 71 for more on the cross stick technique.)

Reversing the Ride Beat on the Hi-Hat (Four Bars)

Ex. 11

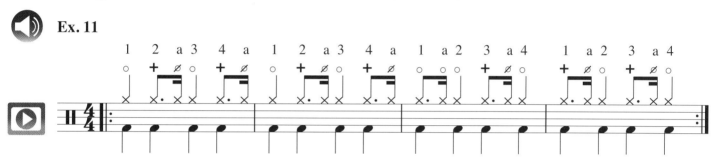

Reversing the Ride Beat on the Hi-Hat (Two Bars)

Ex. 12

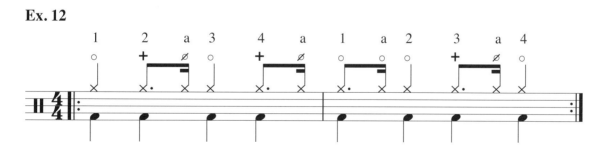

DEVELOPING THE FUNK BASS DRUM

Play the following cymbal and snare patterns against the bass drum patterns in Exercises 1–8.

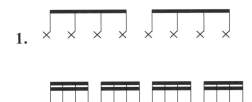

NOTE: Play the hi-hat on 2 and 4. Then practice with the hi-hat on all four beats.

 Ex. 1

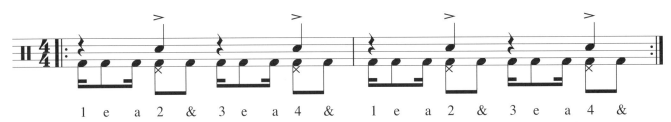

1 e a 2 & 3 e a 4 & 1 e a 2 & 3 e a 4 &

Ex. 2

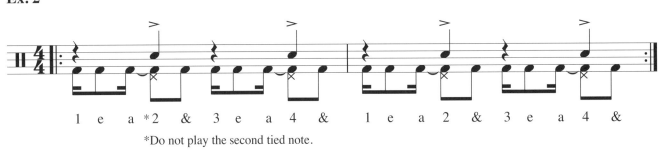

1 e a *2 & 3 e a 4 & 1 e a 2 & 3 e a 4 &

*Do not play the second tied note.

Ex. 3

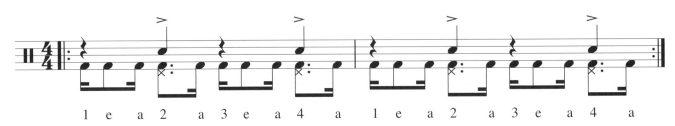

1 e a 2 a 3 e a 4 a 1 e a 2 a 3 e a 4 a

Ex. 4

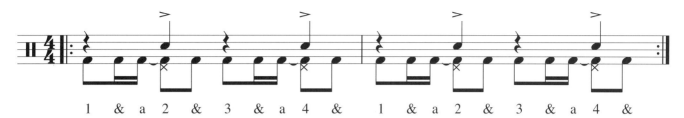

1 & a 2 & 3 & a 4 &   1 & a 2 & 3 & a 4 &

Ex. 5

1 & a 2 e a 3 & a 4 e a   1 & a 2 e a 3 & a 4 e a

Ex. 6

1 & a 2 e & 3 & a 4 e &   1 & a 2 e & 3 & a 4 e &

Ex. 7

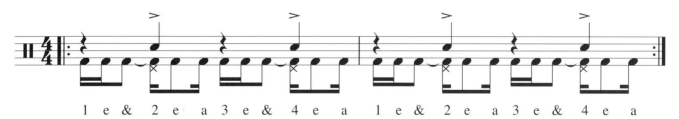

1 e & 2 e a 3 e & 4 e a   1 e & 2 e a 3 e & 4 e a

Ex. 8

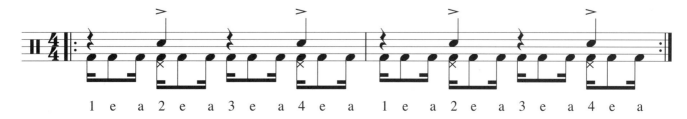

1 e a 2 e a 3 e a 4 e a   1 e a 2 e a 3 e a 4 e a

DEVELOPING THE OPEN HI-HAT SOUND

Ex. 1   Effective use of the hi-hat in contemporary drumming requires learning to control the open sound. When playing the open (○) hi-hat, open the cymbals just wide enough so they are lightly touching each other. Note that the snare drum is on 2 and 4. A good funk and rock drummer should master this technique. Bass drum parts are suggestions only; go ahead and improvise these.

After learning each exercise individually, practice combining two at a time.

Ex. 2   Play the same exercise in sixteenths. Notice that the hi-hat stays open for the duration of two sixteenths. Improvise your own bass drum pattern.

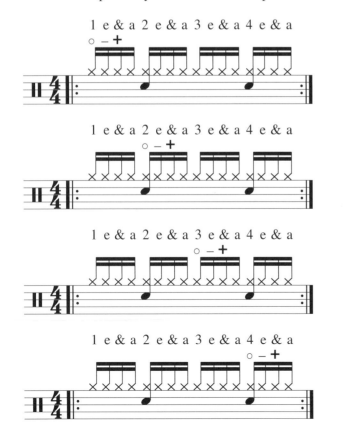
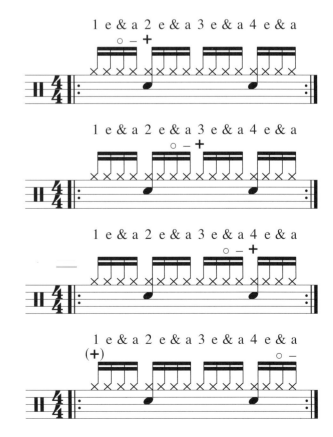

Ex. 3   To really perfect hi-hat control, learn to shift the open hi-hat sound to each succeeding sixteenth. Follow the written examples, then apply the same technique for beats 3 and 4.

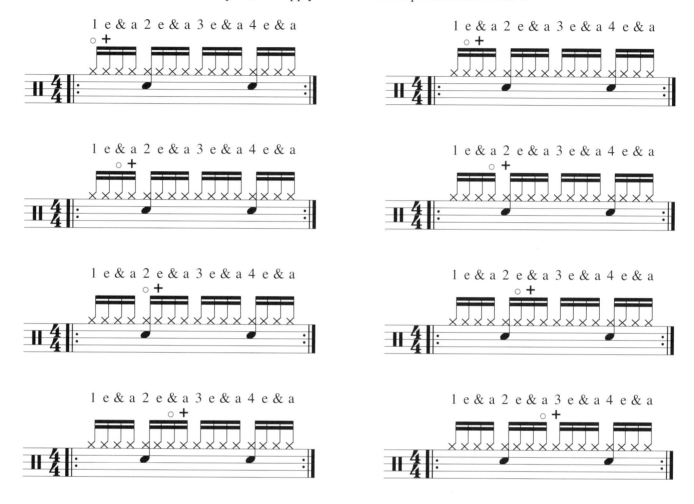

Playing the Hi-Hat with Both Hands

Try the hand techniques below with funk bass drum (Ex. 1) and hi-hat patterns (Ex. 2). Play the sixteenth note hi-hat pattern with both sticks on the hi-hat.

Ex. 4   The first sticking is common for the open-and-closed hi-hat technique. For the second sticking, notice the snare drum is played with the right hand while the left hand keeps the sixteenths flowing.

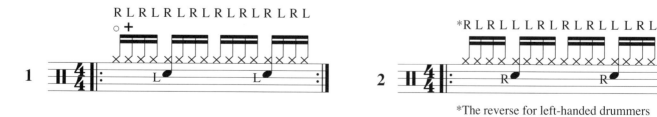

*The reverse for left-handed drummers

LEARNING TO IMPROVISE AROUND THE DRUMSET

A STUDY FOR THE DRUMSET IN SIXTEENTH NOTES

This lesson uses sixteenth notes and multiple sticking patterns. Follow the step-by-step plan and soon the solos will begin developing in your own style.

The Single Stroke

Ex. 1   To start, play sixteenth notes with a steady hand-to-hand motion. The bass drum is played on all four beats, with the hi-hat on 2 and 4.

At first, play these single strokes on the snare drum only. Play a solid forte, the hands alternating from the wrist with a relaxed but exaggerated turn. Practice at a slow tempo to begin with, then a medium tempo, and then a faster tempo. After you feel comfortable at all three tempos on the snare drum (or snare drum pad), repeat the procedure around the drumset (snare and tom-toms). Be sure to keep the sixteenths even and steady.

The Double Stroke

Ex. 2   With double strokes, be sure to let the sticks bounce evenly, keeping the hands relaxed in order to play with maximum speed.

Remember, play first on the snare drum, then around the set.

The Paradiddle

Ex. 3   Singles and doubles are the two most important basic techniques for this method. Once you feel comfortable with your single and double technique, proceed to the rudiment that combines both… the paradiddle.

To develop the paradiddle to a smooth, fast tempo, play the natural accent that falls on the first beat of each paradiddle. The double strokes should be bounced in order to attain maximum speed.

Once you can play these three basic rudiments in all tempos and volumes, proceed to the next step in the method.

Single-Plus-Double Combination Exercise

Ex. 4   Start at a slow tempo. Keep the sixteenths even.

You will notice that the accent comes on every third sixteenth. Without the feet playing, the sixteenths would sound like accented triplets. That is why it is important to play the sixteenths with exact evenness in relation to the feet. The accents form a polyrhythm to the basic time (more on the concept of polyrhythms to come).

Develop the hands carefully so each can play the single and double with equal control. The doubles should be bounce strokes. Once you have developed both the right hand lead and the left hand lead to their potential, proceed to the next step.

Practice this exercise with the feet playing a steady 4/4.

Right hand lead

Left hand lead

Alternating the Single-Plus-Double Combination Exercise

Ex. 5 In order to develop the exercise into a practical tool for improvising around the drumset, you must now learn to alternate the single and double strokes from one hand to the other without interrupting the flow of the sixteenth notes. This is accomplished by adding the paradiddle or an extra double stroke to the exercise which automatically reverses the sticking.

Shifting the hands by adding the paradiddle

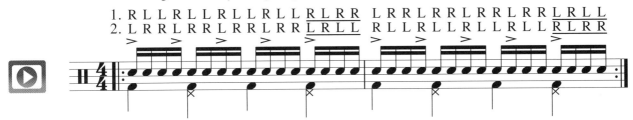

Ex. 6 First learn the exercises as written. After you feel comfortable with the two methods of shifting the singles and doubles from one hand to the other, do it at random. Start the single-plus-double exercise with either hand, and then shift to the other hand by one of the two above methods. Improvise back and forth between the hands. Notice that you can shift the accented singles at will and create interesting accented patterns without disturbing the flow of the sixteenth notes.

Shifting hands by adding an extra double

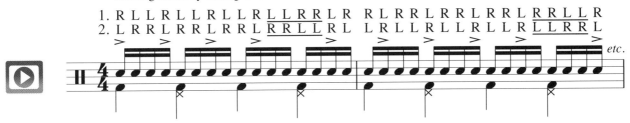

Ex. 7 The following exercise is a short example of how to shift the accents and alternate the singles and doubles between the hands. Use this as a guide to doing the same in a free improvisation on the snare drum. When executed properly, your improvisation should sound like a smooth drum solo in sixteenths with accents.

Improvising on the Snare Drum

Ex. 8 * You may also include straight singles…   and doubles…

*Improvise on the snare drum using the single-plus-double combination. Try to create interesting melodic rhythm patterns with the shifting accents.

… and the paradiddle.

Practice at a slow tempo, a medium tempo, and a fast tempo. Include the bass drum and hi-hat. After you have developed the ability to improvise in sixteenths on the snare drum, it is a simple procedure to move the sixteenths around the snare and tom-toms.

Improvising Around the Drumset

Ex. 9 First experiment with putting the doubles (of the single and double combinations) on the toms while the single remains on the snare.

**Reverse the sticking and play the same exercise starting with the left hand. The double right should now be played on the floor tom-tom.

Ex. 10 Now reverse the procedure. Put the single strokes on the toms and the doubles on the snare.

Play all the combinations from the previous exercises, improvising in sixteenths around the drumset.
Include: Single-plus-double combination strokes alternating hands and accents. Put the doubles on the toms or singles on the toms. Move smoothly from hand to hand and keep the quarters on the feet and the sixteenths even and steady. Listen to all the combinations of drums and accents that you can now play. Notice how easy it is to move around the set in any direction. It is important to stay relaxed while playing. You may also include the single strokes, double strokes, and the paradiddle in your improvisation.

AROUND THE SET IN TRIPLETS

This exercise uses triplets with step-by-step sticking progressions. Follow the same format as you did with the sixteenths. Play the bass drum on all four beats and the hi-hat on the second and fourth beats throughout.

If you want to take these exercises a step further, change them to sixteenth note triplets and play them at a slower speed with an eighth note time feel.

Count triplets as follows:

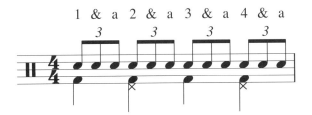

First, play on the snare drum, then around the set.

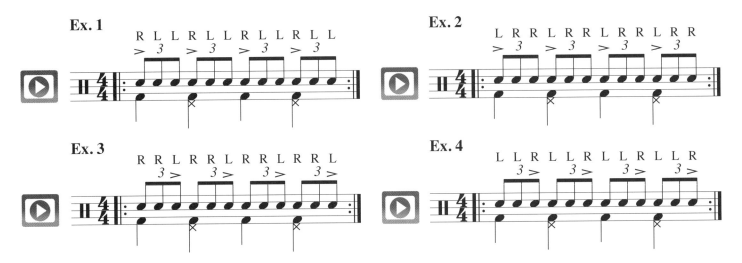

Shifting the Hands

In order to shift the hands from one triplet to another, use a single stroke triplet in the following manner (play the bass drum on all four beats and the hi-hat on beats 2 and 4).

Use these exercises as a guide to switching the hands and the accents. Improvise your own patterns around the drumset using the same techniques. First, play on the snare drum, then around the set.

Ex. 7

Ex. 8

Adding the Double Stroke Triplet and the Paratriplet

To complete the triplet soloing cycle and improvising concept, play the triplets in double strokes and paradiddles.

Triplet in Double Strokes

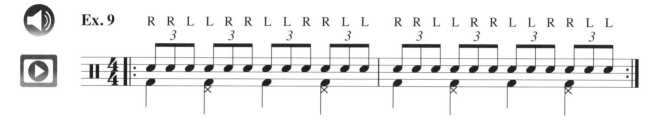

Ex. 9

Triplet in Paradiddles

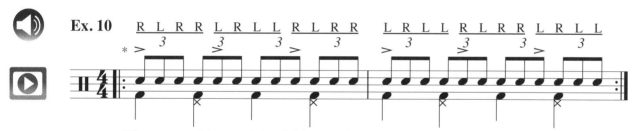

Ex. 10

*The accents of the paratriplets fall in the polyrhythm 3 against 4.

Starting with the Left Hand

Ex. 11

Add the above exercise to previously learned techniques, and practice soloing around the drumset in triplets. Listen carefully and make up your own patterns as you go.

Different Pattern Using Doubles and Singles

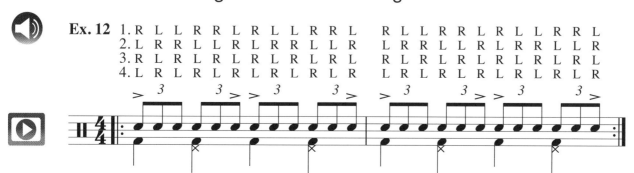

Ex. 12

1. R L L R R L R L L R R L   R L L R R L R L L R R L
2. L R R L L R L R R L L R   L R R L L R L R R L L R
3. R L R L R L R L R L R L   R L R L R L R L R L R L
4. L R L R L R L R L R L R   L R L R L R L R L R L R

BASS DRUM CONTROL

Adding the Bass Drum to the Single-Plus-Double Combination Exercise in Sixteenths

 Ex. 1 Play the following exercises on the snare drum, then around the tom-toms using the different suggested sticking patterns. Practice the sticking patterns **until each two-beat segment** is thoroughly learned.

Master this bar and both sticking patterns
before going on.

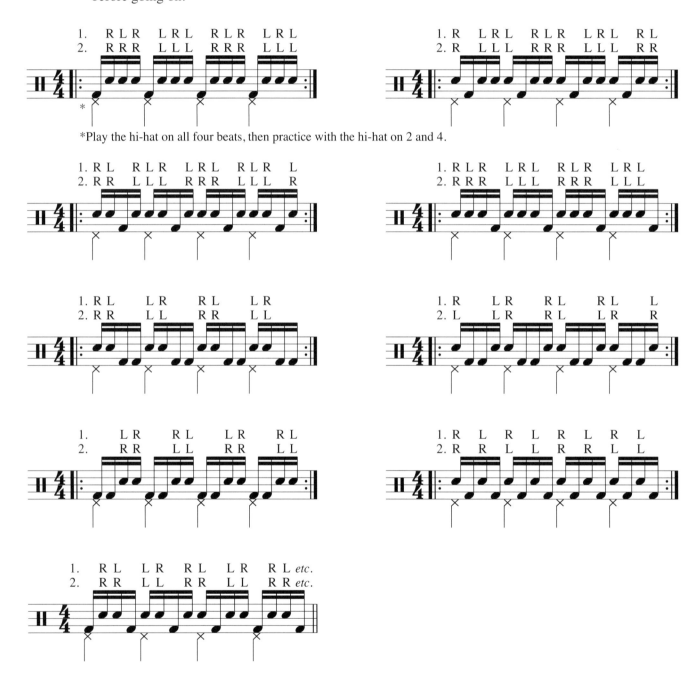

*Play the hi-hat on all four beats, then practice with the hi-hat on 2 and 4.

Improvise around the set using the hand and bass drum combinations. After you are comfortable with the hand and foot combinations, feel free to add single strokes, double strokes, paradiddles, and single-plus-double combinations to the improvisation.

Adding the Bass Drum to the Single-Plus-Double Combination Exercise in Triplets

Ex. 2

*Play the hi-hat on 2 and 4, then practice with the hi-hat on all four beats.

Improvise around the set using all the previous triplet combinations.

PATTERNS AND THE CYMBAL RIDE

Playing the Sixteenth Patterns Against the Ride Cymbal

Here the cymbal ride is played with a tight sixteenth note as written to fit the sixteenths below. Play the hi-hat on all four beats of the bar. Then practice with the hi-hat on 2 and 4.

Ex. 1

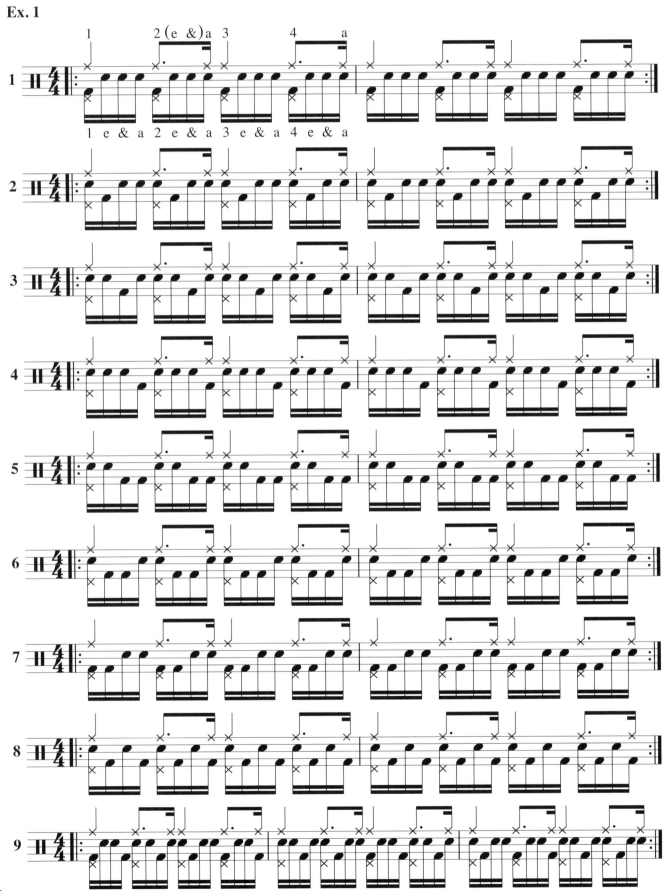

Playing the Triplet Patterns Against the Ride Cymbal

Ex. 2   Here the cymbal ride is played in triplets. Play the hi-hat on beats 2 and 4 while practicing the exercises.

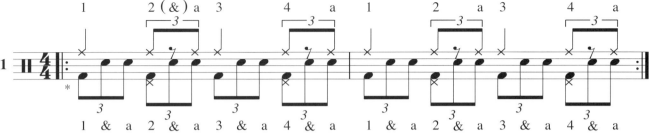

*You may also want to try these exercises with the hi-hat playing the bass drum line while the bass drum plays steady four.

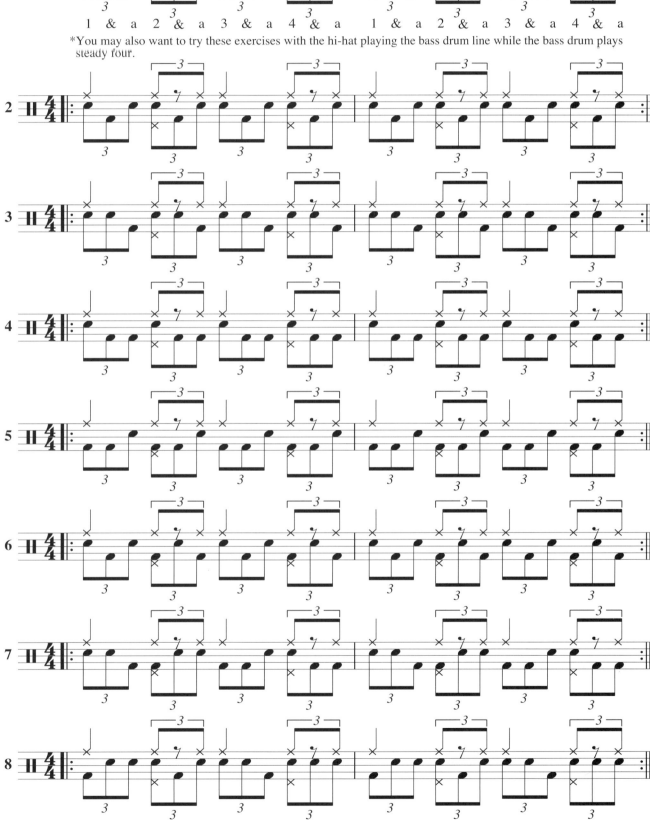

Solo with Techniques So Far

FUSION

Fusion is a modern day rhythmic marriage of three component elements:

- Jazz as played in the swing and be-bop context with a slight rhythmic variation

- Latin in the Afro-Cuban and South American styles

- Contemporary style rock, funk, etc., with a straight eighth note cymbal ride rhythm and a heavy snare drum "back beat" on 2 and 4. (Later in this study, rock will also be explained with the half time feel... fast tempo quarter with the back beat on 3.)

Simply stated, fusion equals **jazz** + **Latin** + **rock**, blended together in a manner that permits the knowledgeable drummer to create new dimensions in time.

Let's begin with…

LATIN RHYTHMS

In learning about Latin rhythms, and all other rhythms for that matter, it's helpful to understand the roots of the rhythms and the cultures that produced them. For an example of how jazz and Latin rhythms began, examine the partial West African drum ensemble as transcribed for the drumset.

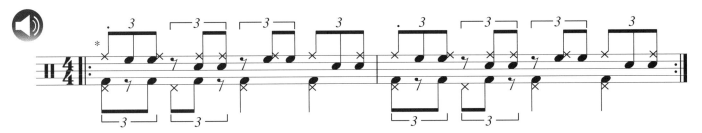

*Keep snares off on the snare drum.

Latin American music originates from two main sources:

- The Afro-Cuban music of the islands in the West Indies (especially Cuba and Puerto Rico

- South America, primarily Brazil and Argentina

While South American drummers play their music at the drumset, rhythm sections of the Caribbean rely primarily on the use of timbales and conga drums for their main driving force. Bongos, claves, guiro (gourd), and other Latin accessory instruments are also widely used in addition to piano and bass.

Jazz drummers have been applying Latin flavors to jazz for years, and contemporary Latin-rock and salsa bands have used rock ideas with Latin influences to add a distinctive sound to their music.

> The following exercises are written in the traditional dance forms of the music. However, they may also be utilized as a base for improvisation on Latin themes.

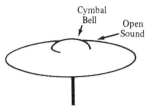

AFRO-CUBAN SALSA RHYTHMS

Cuban Mambo Pattern

 Ex. 1 The rhythms of the mambo are authentically played on the timbales and conga drums. This is an important, sophisticated Afro-Cuban dance rhythm. When transferred to the drumset, the cymbal and cymbal bell can be a substitute for the Latin cowbell, while the snare drum and tom-tom provide the basic conga drum feel.

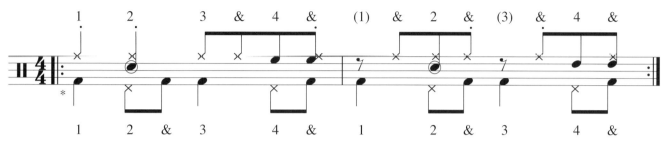

*Bass drum samba part not normally played with Afro-Cuban rhythms

Exercise Breakdown

Notes with a dot above them are played on the bell of the cymbal with the shoulder of the stick; the natural note is played just behind the bell of the cymbal. Start slowly and gradually increase the tempo.

Play the cymbal

Add the bass drum and hi-hat

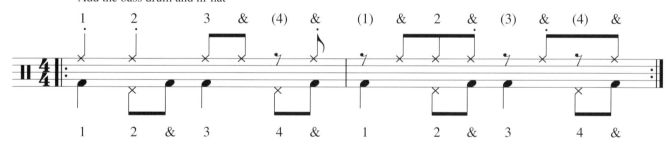

Hold the stick backwards in the matched grip position. Play the snare drum with the butt across the rim as the stick tip is on the drum head—a snare drum cross-stick. A cross-stick is shown in the notation as a snare note with a circle around it. Use the small and medium tom-toms directly above the snare drum, and hit them in the middle of the drum head.

Add the snare drum and tom-tom

Here are two alternate bass drum patterns:

1. Baião (better)

2. Tumbao (best) - Afro-Cuban drummers will use this version more than the others.

Cascara

The cascara rhythm is a rhythm that a timbale player uses to play time, often when accompanying a conga drum solo. The cascara rhythm was traditionally played on the side (or shell) of the timbale. The cascara works well as an interesting drumset rhythm, and variations of this rhythm can be heard on many contemporary recordings.

Ex. 2 Here are a few variations of the cascara to practice. **NOTE:** The cascara pattern may be played on the cowbell, floor tom shell, the cymbal bell, or the open cymbal.

*Alternate rhumba clave rhythm on beat 4 &

More Cymbal (or Cowbell) Variations

 Ex. 3   The bass drum, hi-hat, snare drum, and tom-tom patterns remain the same.

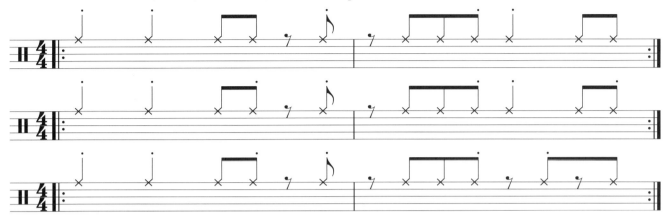

BRAZILIAN RHYTHMS

Bossa Nova

 Ex. 1   The cymbal rhythm can be played on the closed hi-hat or the ride cymbal. The snare drum part is played is played with a cross-stick. **NOTE:** To play a very fast bossa nova, leave the ride pattern out when the cross-stick hits.

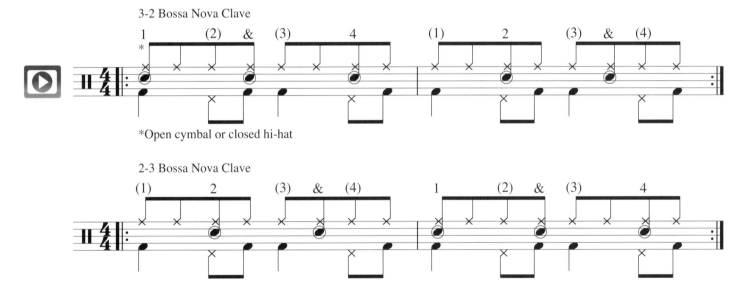

3-2 Bossa Nova Clave

*Open cymbal or closed hi-hat

2-3 Bossa Nova Clave

Samba

 Ex. 2   The samba pattern in this variation is played entirely on the snare drum and should eventually be executed in a fast tempo. The accents are important in attaining the proper feel for this rhythm.

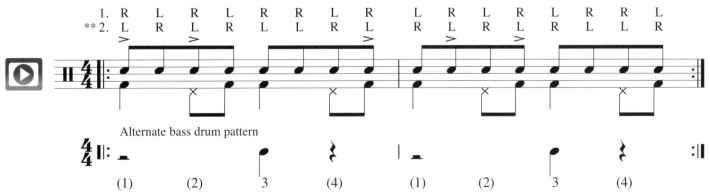

Alternate bass drum pattern

**After learning the samba with the right hand lead, you should then practice it with the left hand leading, i.e., reverse sticking.

Samba Variations in Sixteenths

Ex. 3   Medium tempo samba feel

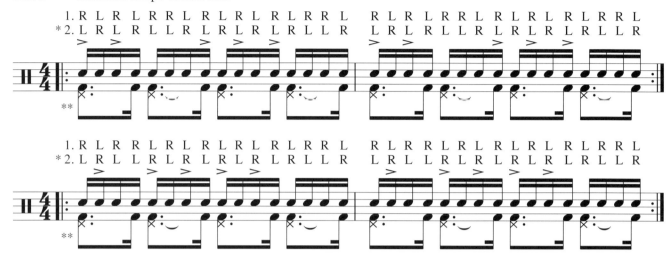

*Optional: Learn to play the above exercises starting with the opposite hand.
   **Play the hi-hat on all four beats while slightly splashing on beats 2 and 4 (indicated by the ties).

Brazilian Samba Pattern with Ride Cymbal and Snare Drum

 Ex. 4   Play the jazz ride straight (not swung) on the ride cymbal or the hi-hat (open and close on 2 and 4) while the left hand plays the samba pattern on the snare drum. The cymbal pattern is in open eighth notes to fit the rhythmic character of the samba beat.

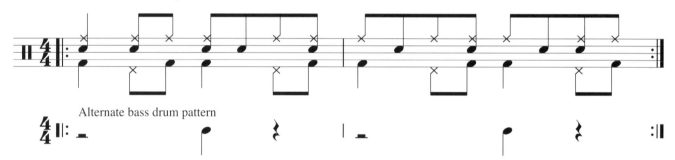

Alternate bass drum pattern

Exercise Breakdown

Play the cymbal ride on the ride cymbal or the hi-hat

Add the bass drum and hi-hat

Add the snare drum

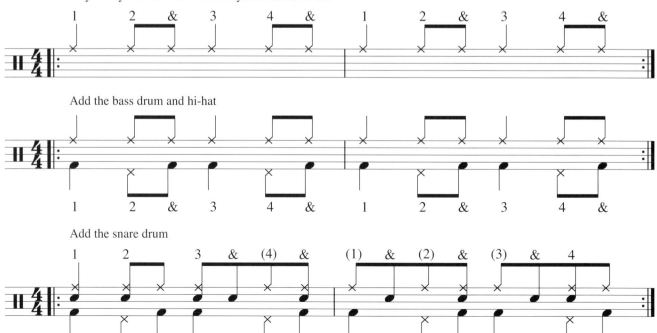

Ex. 5 A more contemporary variation on the same feel

HALF TIME LATIN FUNK-ROCK FEEL

 Ex. 1 Contemporary drummers have added a rock beat to the Latin influence resulting in a hybrid style of Latin rock. Here is a Latin theme written between the snare drum and cymbal which combines Latin with the rock beat on 3.

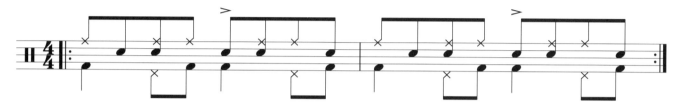

Exercise Breakdown

Play the ride cymbal (on the open cymbal or the cymbal bell)

Add the snare drum (accent on beat 3)

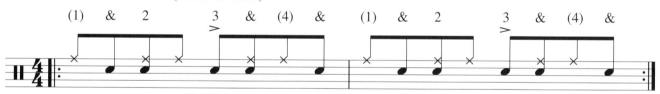

Add the bass drum and hi-hat

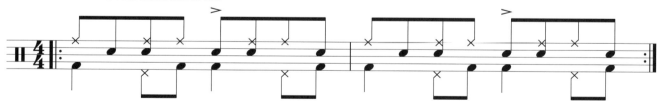

Ex. 2 Example of the same exercise written at half the tempo.

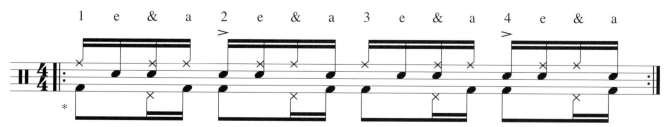

*Also, improvise your own bass drum patterns.

HALF TIME ROCK FEEL

Ex. 3   Here's a standard rock beat presented in a half time feel.

Below, the same pattern takes one bar because the note values have been halved.

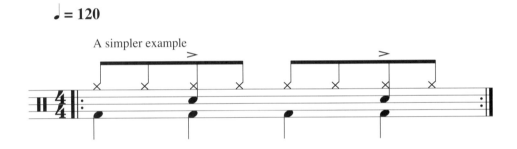

Understanding this concept is important to fusion because fusion is a mixture of jazz, Latin, and rock played at a faster tempo. This is the best way to understand how the rock feel fits in at the fusion tempo.

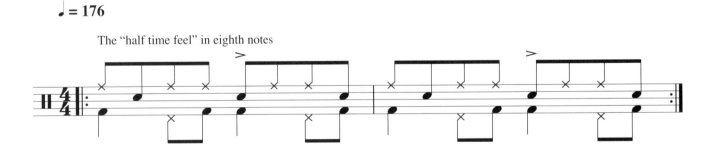

JAZZ RIDE IN EIGHTHS

As mentioned earlier, the jazz ride with a slight rhythmic variation from the normal triplet pattern is also an essential element of the fusion concept. The triplet jazz ride should now be played in eighth notes. (Use the same elbow and stick motion as the triplet version if that method works for you.)

Ex. 1

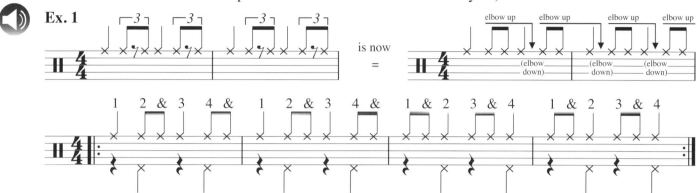

Practice these eighth note jazz ride variations with the hi-hat on 2 and 4 and the hi-hat on all four. Improvise your own bass drum and snare drum patterns.

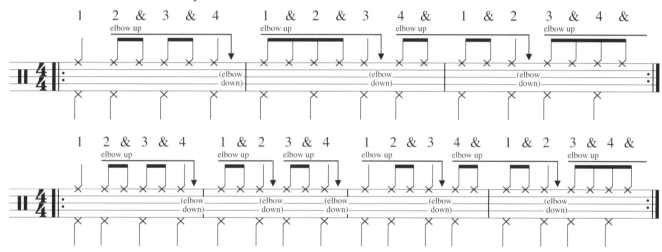

Putting It All Together

The Changing Groove Exercise

Ex. 2   **NOTE:** The tempo remains the same throughout the exercise. Also practice the same exercise with eight bars of time and a four-bar fill.

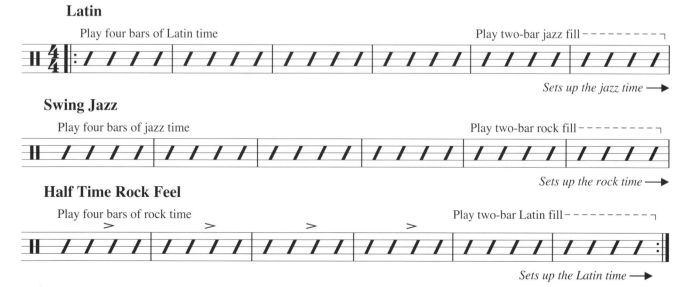

TWO-BAR DRUM FILLS

In the preceding exercise, the different sections should be played in the authentic rhythmic feel of the basic patterns. The function of the two-bar fills (solos) is to set up each new section. Here are some examples of two-bar fills for each rhythmic category. Learn these, then improvise your own.

In the Jazz Feel

Ex. 1

In the Rock Feel

Ex. 2

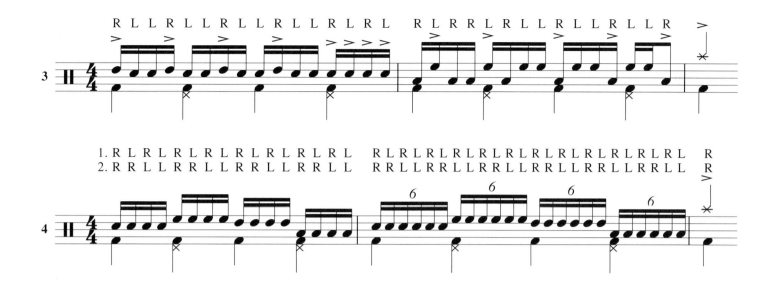

In the Latin Feel

I like to think of Latin fills as played on the timbales. A timbale drummer plays syncopated rim shots combined with the open sound of the drums. The strokes are played hard, and the rhythm of the fill accentuates the feeling of the Latin time.

Ex. 3

FUSION TIME

Ex. 1

As a starting point, play the bass drum and hi-hat in the following pattern.

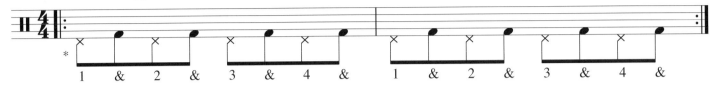

*OPTION: The hi-hat part may also be interpreted as a double bass drum part.

Add the ride cymbal

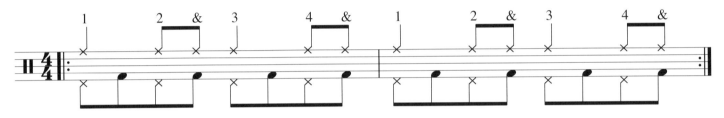

Improvise with the left hand in the following manner.

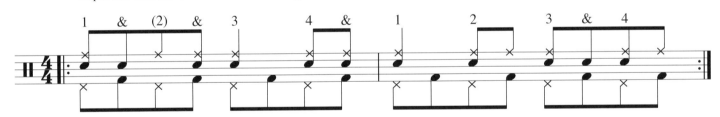

Play the above exercise with the cymbal ride reversed.

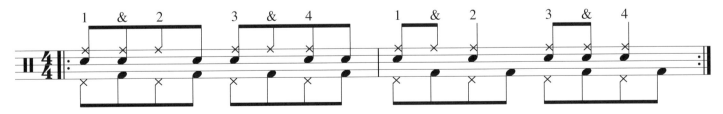

Ex. 2   Here is an example of the ride cymbal pattern mixed with the (open) jazz ride and the Latin feel.

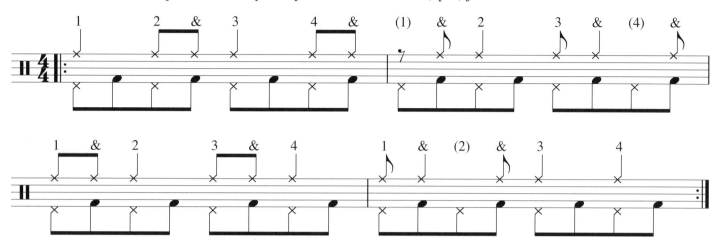

Ex. 3   Another example showing how the mixing of jazz, Latin, and rock ultimately contributes to the fusion concept.

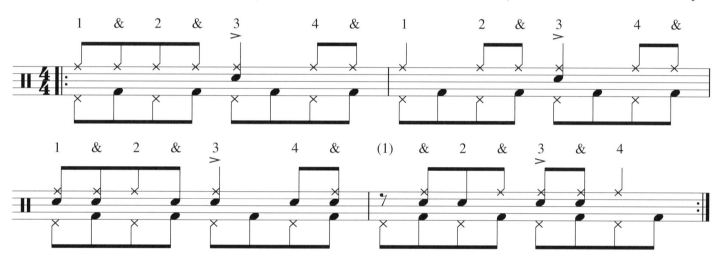

Ex. 4   This example frees up the bass drum (improvise your own snare drum patterns).

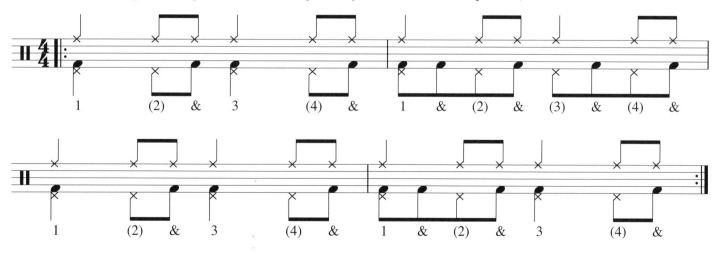

Solo—Putting It All Together

Improvise fusion time with a smooth, steady flow. Try different tempos and incorporate all the ideas you can when practicing.

FLAMS AND FLAM BEATS

In review, one of the best and oftentimes most misunderstood rudiments for playing exchanges between the hands are flam rudiments and their variations.

The Flam

The main note is played immediately after the grace note. The hand playing the grace note will always be closer to the drum head. When one flam is played, the hands reverse so the hand that played the main note now will play the grace note. Always aim to keep the grace note hand still and close to the drum when you are switching hands for the next flam.

Right-Handed Flam   Left-Handed Flam

The Flam Tap

Play each of the following flam rudiments on the snare drum.

Ex. 1

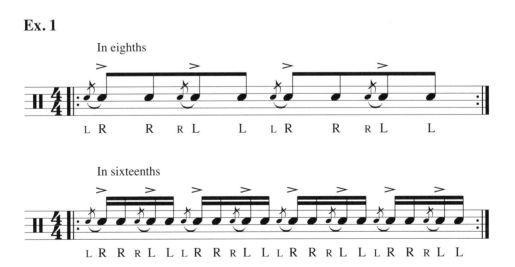

Then separate the hands and play the right hand on the ride cymbal and the left hand on the snare drum.* Play the bass drum in four and the hi-hat on 2 and 4. Notice that when you're playing with the right hand on the ride cymbal and the left hand on the snare drum an interesting independent rhythm occurs between the two hands, creating a stereo effect.

*The reverse for left-handed drummers

The Flam Paradiddle

Ex. 2

L R L R R R L R L L L R L R R R L R L L

When playing the flam paradiddle between the right hand (ride cymbal) and left hand (snare drum), accent the left hand flam on 2 and 4 and give it a funk feel.

Once you have become comfortable playing flam beats with the hands separated, improvise (including more with the bass drum) so you are actually playing a "flam-funk" rhythm. Play the hi-hat on 2 and 4 and on all four quarters to the bar.

Here is a flam combination that alternates the flam to the same hand as the last sixteenth. This is an unnatural way of playing flam exercises. However, listen to the interesting rhythmic pattern when played with the hands separated.

L R L R L R L R L R L R L R L R L R L R L R L R

Improvise in sixteenth note flams between the ride cymbal and snare drum. Play the hi-hat on all four beats, and include the bass drum in your improvisations.

Flams in Triplets

Ex. 3   Triplet flams accommodate the jazz feel. Practice the patterns on the snare drum, then with the hands separated between the ride cymbal and the snare drum.

L R L R R R L R L L L R L R R R L R L

L R R R L L L R R R L L L R R R L L

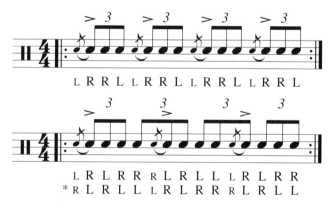

L R R L L L R R L L L R R L L L R R L

L R L R R R L R L L L R L R R
*R L R L L L R L R R R L R L L

*Stickings will be the opposite on the repeat.

Improvise a flam triplet solo.

More Flam Beats in Sixteenths

Ex. 4

L R L L L R R L R R L L R L L L R R L R R L

L R R L R R L L R L R L L R L L L R R L R

1. L R R L L L R R L L R R L L R R L L R R L L R etc.
2. R L L R R L L R R L L R R L L R R L L R R L etc.

83

PRACTICAL MUSICIANSHIP 🔊

Auditions

When seeking employment, auditions often become a factor. The best approach is to avoid overplaying. Simply relax and play positive, steady time to show your maturity and musicianship… you'll have a better chance of getting the job. You can show the total scope of your playing ability at a more appropriate time.

Click Track

The click track is a professional metronome that is often used in recording studios. The drummer and the rest of the musicians have to perform the music exactly to the tempo of the click, which is heard through headphones.

Music Terms & Symbols

    ⊕ Coda Sign; indicates an extended ending

    a tempo back to the original tempo

    D.C. back to the top (da capo)

    D.S. back to the sign (dal segno)

    𝄋 the D.S. sign

    ⌢ Fermata; hold the note or rest that is under a fermata sign

    // Pause; means to come to a sudden stop

    tacet do not play

    v.s. watch for a fast page turn

Equipment Selection

Cymbals: Since cymbals are the personality of the drummer's sound, great care should be taken in their selection. If possible, strike each cymbal with sticks, mallets, and brushes in order to hear all the "colors" of each cymbal before making a final choice.

Drumsticks: Drumsticks should not be too heavy or too light. Practicing with steel drumsticks or extra heavy wooden sticks is not beneficial to your overall technique. You want to develop strength with speed, not bulk. To achieve this, practice on the live drum or a practice pad with your normal playing drumstick or a slightly heavier concert snare drumstick. When purchasing drumsticks, match the sound of each stick by striking the countertop lightly. Make sure the sticks are not warped by gently rolling them across the countertop.

Endurance

Drums are physical instruments and make varying demands depending on the type of music you are playing. The shape you are in should be equal to the energy required by your music. When your endurance gives out, your playing suffers. (See Speed and Power on page 92.)

Fills

The drum fill, as explained earlier in the book, is the drummer's way of injecting excitement as well as "setting up" important phrases for the other musicians. This short improvised solo can also make the listener aware of the drummer's technique and dexterity around the drumset. There is a tendency for some drummers to "overplay" drum fills and forget about their musical purpose. When playing a drum fill, play with authority, command, and musical taste. This will impress the listener as well as your fellow musicians.

Fast Tempos

One of the professional drummer's most demanding physical and technical feats is the ability to maintain fast tempos for long periods of time. In your practice schedule, include playing time and soloing at fast tempos in order to be in shape for the real thing.

Form

Most music is comprised of musical phrases that recur in a repetitive order. This is called form. A knowledge of musical form will enable you to more easily add fills at points of climax and in the transition of phrases. Examples of common forms:

Blues—12-Bar Basic Blues

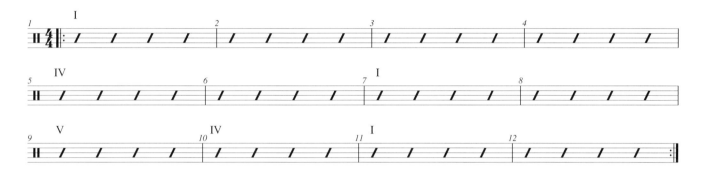

Standard (Jazz) Tune A A B A

- First (A) is eight bars
- Second (A) is the same eight bars repeated
- (B) is eight bars but a different melody
- Last (A) is the same as the first (A)

Asymmetrical Time

In 4/4 we have a balanced number of beats. The same applies to 2/4, cut time (¢ or 2/2), and 6/8. Asymmetrical (odd) time is a meter with an irregular number of beats, i.e., 3/4, 5/4, 5/8, 7/4, etc. To play and improvise in an odd time, simply apply what you know from even time, changing your thinking to fit 5 or 7 or 3.

Recording

Your drums may have to be muffled and tuned differently when doing a studio recording. Also, to avoid your sound "leaking" into the microphones of other musicians, you may have to be isolated. This sometimes necessitates using headphones. The suggestions from engineers and producers to achieve the best sound from the drums should be taken seriously.

When playing, stay relaxed and concentrate on the music. You may have to do one segment over a few times until everything is right. Be prepared to play 100% for as many times as it takes to achieve the desired results.

Playing Experience

To gain confidence in your own playing ability, it is important to gain playing experience. In order to do this, spend as much time as possible listening to other drummers and musicians you enjoy. Organize your own playing sessions and "sit in" with other bands when you are asked to do so. I have also found it helpful to play along with recordings when live playing situations are not readily available.

ADDITIONAL SKILLS AND TECHNIQUES

Brushes

Most drummers who play brushes well have distinctive styles. The art of brush playing takes practice to master. Here's a start. Play the left brush from left to right sweeping it across the drum head in a long oval. The outside strokes are on beats 1 and 3; the inside strokes are on beats 2 and 4.

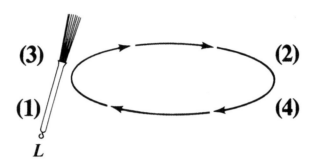

The right brush crosses over the sweeping brush and plays the jazz ride beat like this:

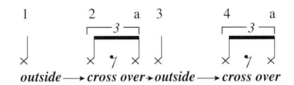

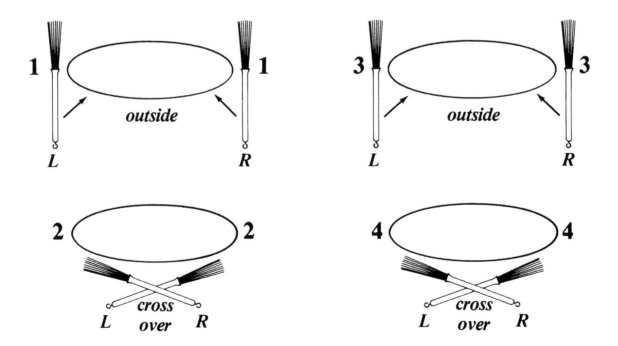

When accenting with brushes, slap the brush and the (covered) brush handle off the snare drum rim at the same time in order to achieve a loud brush pop. Accenting occurs while the brushes are moving in a continuous flow.

Buzz Roll

The buzz roll, often referred to as the closed or press roll, is a series of buzz sounds from each alternating stick.

To begin developing your buzz roll, play a short, relaxed buzz with each stick. Be careful not to tense your hands as you play.

After you can play a clear buzz in each hand, increase the speed until the buzz connects into one continuous sound.

Start a buzz roll very softly. The hands should move just fast enough to connect the buzz of each alternating stick. The amount of stick pressure should be the weight of the drumstick only.

Once you have attained an even, smooth, soft roll, begin to apply pressure to the stick. Add the pressure by tightening the grip of the index finger and thumb of both hands in matched grip. (For the traditional grip, tighten the index finger and thumb of the right hand and the thumb only of the left hand.) At the same time you are tightening your grip, press harder into the drum head.

When you add pressure to the roll, the duration of the buzz is shorter. To keep the roll connected and smooth, increase the speed of the alternating hands. Practice this exercise for one or two minutes each day to develop a good clean buzz roll.

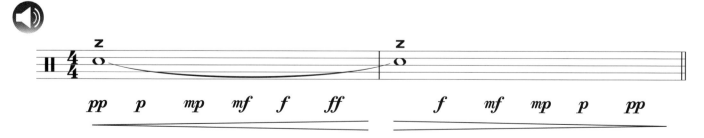

Polyrhythm

A polyrhythm is two different meters played simultaneously.

When polyrhythms don't relate mathematically to each other, they may be called dissonant; when polyrhythms do relate to each other, they may be called consonant. Polyrhythms that do relate to each other are the most musical.

The study of polyrhythms will improve your overall rhythmic concept and sharpen your awareness of time.

4/4 – 1 to 1 ratio (not a polyrhythm). The quarter is then divided into eighths, triplets, and sixteenths:

quarter

eighths

triplets
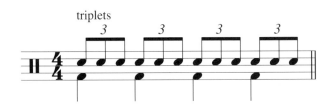

sixteenths

Polyrhythms and how they relate to basic 4/4 time:

3 over 4, a 3/4 to 1 ratio

5 over 4, a 1-1/4 to 1 ratio
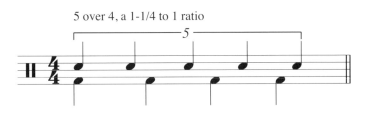

 All polyrhythms can be broken into their component rhythms. I've chosen to show you 6 over 4 (and its subdivisions) because of its comfortable relationship to the 4/4 time signature.

6 over 4, a 1-1/2 to 1 ratio

6 over 4, a 1-1/2 to 1 ratio in eighths
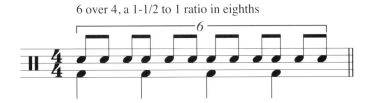

6 over 4, a 1-1/2 to 1 ratio in triplets

6 over 4, a 1-1/2 to 1 ratio in sixteenths
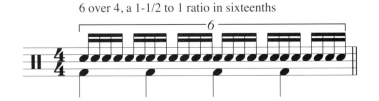

7 over 4, a 1-3/4 to 1 ratio
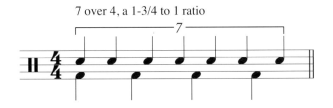

8 over 4, a 2 to 1 ratio (double time)

Polyrhythms in 3/4 time:

Polyrhythm Ratios*

In this context, the word "ratio" refers to the contrasting tempo of a polyrhythm or polymeter as compared to the consistent basic pulse of the time signature from which it is measured.

3 over 4 = 3/4 to 1

4 and 4 = 1 to 1

5 over 4 = 1-1/4 to 1

6 over 4 = 1-1/2 to 1

7 over 4 = 1-3/4 to 1

8 over 4 = 2 to 1

*Peter Magadini is the author of *Polyrhythms: The Musician's Guide*.

Reading the Drum Chart

The drummer's role as time keeper must never be sacrificed for the written note. Steady musical time should always come first. With that in mind, the written drum part is incorporated into the time. This can be initially accomplished by playing the part with the left hand while the time continues on the ride cymbal. This method of independent reading works well for jazz charts if the drummer is not yet an experienced reader.

After the drummer becomes more experienced, drum fills (short solo phrases) that weave around the written notes can be added. These fills, called "set ups," mark the time and expose the written notes so the rest of the band can hit certain notes together. A fill should always add to the music and not detract from it.

 Ex. 1 Play time on the ride cymbal. The written notes are played with the snare drum hand. Play in the jazz triplet time frame or in the even eighth note (fusion) time frame.

Hand-to-hand "choreography" and drum fills are indicated in this drum chart. Practice in both triplet and eighth note styles.

- C – Strike the cymbal and the snare drum at the same time (you should play the C on either the ride cymbal or crash cymbal with either the right or left hand).

- S – Snare drum alone. Notice that fills are indicated even through the rests at times. The drum fill keeps going in order to "set up" a following note.

 Ex. 2 Play time on the ride cymbal. The written notes are played with the snare drum hand. Play in the jazz triplet time frame or in the even eighth note (fusion) time frame.

*A dot under a note indicates a suggested bass drum punch.

**The fills you eventually decide to play could be, and probably should be, your own. The ones that are included here also work perfectly well.

FINAL TIPS

Counting

Counting is an important aspect of a drummer's reading ability because it provides a means for mentally keeping the beats of a bar in place. While it's not necessary to count every time you are reading, it is a helpful assist when you are not sure of a particular part.

Speed and Power

Here's an exercise to increase speed, power, and endurance. It only takes six minutes a day.

The Six Minute Single Stroke Exercise

Play single strokes (alternate strokes) as fast and as loud as possible in the following manner:

1. **Play one minute – rest one minute**

2. **Play 30 seconds – rest 30 seconds**

   Repeat

3. **Play 15 seconds – rest 15 seconds**

   Repeat

4. **Play 5 seconds – rest 5 seconds**

   Play 6 times

Total Playing Time: 3 minutes   **Total Rest Time: 3 minutes**

To keep track of the time, use a clock/watch with a second hand or a metronome set at 60.

Free Improvisation

Sometimes musical circumstances require a drummer who can improvise without form or a time base to follow. Playing "free jazz" or in a musical situation without rules can be exciting and challenging. Even if you never have the opportunity in performance, practicing this concept at the drumset can be musically rewarding.

Begin by playing anything on any drum or part of a drum or cymbal. Use sticks, brushes, mallets, hands, fingers, or any combination of these. Clear your mind of preconceived patterns and try to totally create your own musical environment with new patterns, textures, and sounds.

By including free playing in your practice routine, you'll find that new and creative ideas begin to enhance your playing style. And these will be totally yours!

Warm-Up

Stay relaxed when playing this pattern and let the sticks bounce. Start slowly and gradually increase the tempo to maximum speed; then gradually slow down to the original tempo. Play on the snare drum or practice pad.

1. R L L R R L R L L R R L   R L R L R L R L R L R L   R L R L R L R L R L R L   R L R L R L R L L R R L
*2. L R R L L R L R R L L R   L R L R L R L R L R L R   L R L R L R L R L R L R   L R L R L R L R R L L R

*Sticking pattern may be reversed

CONCLUSION 🔊

When playing, put as much of yourself into the music as possible and enjoy what you are doing. Respond to the music and your fellow musicians with an aware ear, suitable volume, accurate time and, of course, the proper feel.

ABOUT THE AUTHOR

Photo by Armelle deCénival

Peter Magadini, performer, educator and author of international renown, continues to bring a broad spectrum of musical experience with this combo edition of his book *Learn to Play the Drumset*.

As a drummer, Mr. Magadini has played with many familiar artists and organizations, including George Duke Trio, Diana Ross, Bobbie Gentry, Chet Baker, and the John Handy Quintet. As a percussionist, he has performed in the Berkshire Music Festival Orchestra at Tanglewood, the show *Les Misérables*, and the Toronto Symphony Orchestra.

In addition, Peter has performed as a studio musician in Los Angeles, Toronto, Montreal, and San Francisco. He has been recorded on several major labels and has four recordings under his own name. Peter has also authored two of the very first books on the subject of polyrhythms. His book *Polyrhythms—The Musician's Guide* (Hal Leonard) was voted #6 in the *Modern Drummer* magazine survey of "the greatest 25 drum books" and he has received critical acclaim for his book *Polyrhythms for the Drumset* (Alfred) and his DVD *Jazz Drums* (Hal Leonard).

A well-qualified educator, Peter has taught at the Los Angeles Professional Drum Shop, the San Francisco Conservatory of Music, McGill and Concordia Universities (Canada), and the Dave Brubeck Institute (San Francisco Bay area). He continues to teach privately at his own studio and is offering limited international study online.

Peter holds degrees from both the San Francisco Conservatory of Music (BM Percussion) and the University of Toronto (MM Percussion).

www.petermagadini.com

YOU CAN'T BEAT OUR DRUM BOOKS!

Learn to Play the Drumset – Book 1
by Peter Magadini

This unique method starts students out on the entire drumset and teaches them the basics in the shortest amount of time. Book 1 covers basic 4- and 5-piece set-ups, grips and sticks, reading and improvisation, coordination of hands and feet, and features a variety of contemporary and basic rhythm patterns with exercise breakdowns for each.

06620030 Book/CD Pack... $14.99

Creative Timekeeping For The Contemporary Jazz Drummer
by Rick Mattingly

Combining a variety of jazz ride cymbal patterns with coordination and reading exercises, *Creative Timekeeping* develops true independence: the ability to play any rhythm on the ride cymbal while playing any rhythm on the snare and bass drums. It provides a variety of jazz ride cymbal patterns as well as coordination and reading exercises that can be played along with them. Five chapters: Ride Cymbal Patterns; Coordination Patterns and Reading; Combination Patterns and Reading; Applications; and Cymbal Reading.

06621764 .... $9.99

The Drumset Musician
by Rod Morgenstein and Rick Mattingly

Containing hundreds of practical, usable beats and fills, The Drumset Musician teaches you how to apply a variety of patterns and grooves to the actual performance of songs. The accompanying CD includes demos as well as 14 play-along tracks covering a wide range of rock, blues and pop styles, with detailed instructions on how to create exciting, solid drum parts.

06620011 Book/CD Pack... $19.99

Drum Aerobics
by Andy Ziker

A 52-week, one-exercise-per-day workout program for developing, improving, and maintaining drum technique. Players of all levels – beginners to advanced – will increase their speed, coordination, dexterity and accuracy. The online audio contains all 365 workout licks, plus play-along grooves in styles including rock, blues, jazz, heavy metal, reggae, funk, calypso, bossa nova, march, mambo, New Orleans 2nd Line, and lots more!

06620137 Book/Online Audio $19.99

40 Intermediate Snare Drum Solos
For Concert Performance
by Ben Hans

This book provides the advancing percussionist with interesting solo material in all musical styles. It is designed as a lesson supplement, or as performance material for recitals and solo competitions. Includes: 40 intermediate snare drum solos presented in easy-to-read notation; a music glossary; Percussive Arts Society rudiment chart; suggested sticking, dynamics and articulation markings; and much more!

06620067 .... $7.99

Joe Porcaro's Drumset Method – Groovin' with Rudiments
Patterns Applied to Rock, Jazz & Latin Drumset
by Joe Porcaro

Master teacher Joe Porcaro presents rudiments at the drumset in this sensational new edition of *Groovin' with Rudiments*. This book is chock full of exciting drum grooves, sticking patterns, fills, polyrhythmic adaptations, odd meters, and fantastic solo ideas in jazz, rock, and Latin feels. The enclosed CD features 99 audio clip examples in many styles to round out this true collection of superb drumming material for every serious drumset performer.

06620129 Book/CD Pack... $24.99

Show Drumming
The Essential Guide to Playing Drumset for Live Shows and Musicals
by Ed Shaughnessy and Clem DeRosa

Who better to teach you than "America's Premier Showdrummer" himself, Mr. Ed Shaughnessy! Features: a step-by-step walk-through of a simulated show; CD with music, comments & tips from Ed; notated examples; practical tips; advice on instruments; a special accessories section with photos; and more!

06620080 Book/CD Pack... $16.95

Instant Guide to Drum Grooves
The Essential Reference for the Working Drummer
by Maria Martinez

Become a more versatile drumset player! From traditional Dixieland to cutting-edge hip-hop, Instant Guide to Drum Grooves is a handy source featuring 100 patterns that will prepare working drummers for the stylistic variety of modern gigs. The book includes essential beats and grooves in such styles as: jazz, shuffle, country, rock, funk, New Orleans, reggae, calypso, Brazilian and Latin.

06620056 Book/CD Pack... $10.99

The Complete Drumset Rudiments
by Peter Magadini

Use your imagination to incorporate these rudimental etudes into new patterns that you can apply to the drumset or tom toms as you develop your hand technique with the Snare Drum Rudiments, your hand and foot technique with the Drumset Rudiments and your polyrhythmic technique with the Polyrhythm Rudiments. Adopt them all into your own creative expressions based on ideas you come up with while practicing.

06620016 Book/CD Pack... $14.95

Drum Tuning
The Ultimate Guide
by Scott Schroedl

This book/CD pack is designed for drummers of all styles and levels. It contains step-by-step instruction along with over 35 professional photos that allow you to see the tools and tuning techniques up close. Covers: preparation; drumhead basics; drum construction and head properties; tom-toms; snare drum; bassdrum; the drum set as one instrument; drum sounds and tuning over the years; when to change heads; and more.

06620060 Book/CD Pack... $14.95

HAL•LEONARD®

Prices, contents, and availability
subject to change without notice.

www.halleonard.com

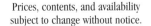

0417